Art Institute of Chicago

Charles Mather Ffoulke Tapestry Collection

1896

Art Institute of Chicago

Charles Mather Ffoulke Tapestry Collection
1896

ISBN/EAN: 9783337149895

Printed in Europe, USA, Canada, Australia, Japan

Cover: Foto ©Andreas Hilbeck / pixelio.de

More available books at **www.hansebooks.com**

THE ANTIQUARIANS OF THE ART INSTITUTE
OF CHICAGO

CATALOGUE

OF A

COLLECTION OF TAPESTRIES

LENT BY

CHARLES M. FFOULKE
OF WASHINGTON, D. C.

JANUARY 1ST TO JANUARY 15TH, 1896

INCLUDING THE
YEAR BOOK OF THE ANTIQUARIANS

———— · ·

CHICAGO
R. R. DONNELLEY & SONS COMPANY, PRINTERS
MDCCCXCVI

THE ANTIQUARIANS OF THE ART INSTITUTE.

OFFICERS:

PRESIDENT,

MRS. JOHN N. JEWETT.

VICE-PRESIDENT,

MRS. JOHN J. GLESSNER.

SECRETARY,

MRS. ROBERT B. GREGORY.

TREASURER,

MRS. DUDLEY WILKINSON.

DIRECTORS,

MRS. J. Y. SCAMMON,	MRS. H. O. STONE,
MRS. S. M. NICKERSON,	MRS. WM. J. CHALMERS,
MRS. O. W. POTTER,	MRS. A. A. SPRAGUE,
MRS. W. W. KIMBALL,	MISS PULLMAN.

The officers and members of the Society of the Antiquarians of the Art Institute take this opportunity of expressing their deep obligations to Mr. Charles M. Ffoulke, of Washington, D. C., for the loan of the magnificent collection of tapestries described in the following pages.

To the enlightened generosity of this distinguished collector, the Antiquarians, the Art Institute and the art-loving public of Chicago owe the opportunity of seeing these rare examples of Textile Art.

Chicago, January 1, 1896.

List of the Tapestries

Twenty-three of the tapestries here exhibited, constituting the Series Constantine, Chateau Series, Series Moses, Series Judith and Series Diana, are from the famous collection of the Barberini Palace In Rome, of which a description will be found upon page 16.

Series Constantine the Great.   6 tapestries.

1. Constantine slaying a lion in gladiatorial combat.—Romanelli or Cortona. For description, see pp. 15, 24.

2. Constantine contemplating the flaming cross in the sky.—Romanelli. For description, see pp. 15, 25.

3. Constantine destroying idols and replacing them with Christian statues.—Cortona.
   For description, see pp. 15, 26.

4. Naval battle between the fleets of Constantine and Licinius in the Bosphorus.—Charles Neapolitan.
   For description, see pp. 15, 26.

5. Constantine burning the creed of the Arians at Nicæa.—Romanelli. For description, see pp. 15, 27.

6. Constantine superintending the construction of Constantinople.—Rubens. For description, see pp. 15, 28.

Series Chateau and Garden Scenes.   4 tapestries.

7. Arbor in two sections supported on eight caryatides.
   For description, see pp. 30, 32.

8. Arbor in parts of three sections supported on four caryatides. For description, see pp. 30, 32.

7

9. Arbor in one section supported on four caryatides.
For description, see pp. 3⁵, 33.

10. Arbor in one section supported on eight caryatides.
For description, see pp. 30, 34.

Series Events in the Life of Moses. 1 tapestry.

11. Moses and his wife, Zipporah, taking care of the lambs of his father in law, Jethro's flock.
For description, see p. 36.

Series Judith and Holofernes. 5 tapestries.

12. King Nebuchadnezzar sends Holofernes, the Chief Captain of his army, against Israel.
For description, see pp. 38, 47, 49.

13. Achior, the leader of the Ammonites, while expounding the power of the God of Israel, is arrested by order of Holofernes. For description see pp. 38, 47, 50

14. Not exhibited. In Florence.
For description, see pp. 38, 47, 50.

15. Judith arrays herself in garments of gladness in order that she may free Bethulia from destruction.
For description, see pp. 38, 48, 51.

16. Judith, in the guise of a fugitive, cunningly deceives Holofernes, and promises him victory.
For description see pp. 38, 48, 51.

17. Holofernes, while drunken, is deprived of his head by Judith, who thus saves Israel.
For description, see pp. 38, 48, 53.

18, 19. Not exhibited. In Florence.
For description, see pp. 38, 48, 54.

Series Diana. 7 tapestries.

Flemish Renaissance Tapestries. 4.

Achilles Series. 2 tapestries.

Series Meleager and Atalanta. 2 tapestries.

Various Tapestries. 6.

Monograph on the Series Constantine the Great.

Composed of Six Tapestries.

Title, Signature, Author of Cartoon and Size of each Tapestry.

No. 1.—Constantine slaying a lion in gladiatorial combat.

> Signed IAC. D. L. RIV. Cartoon attributed by some to Romanelli and by others to Cartona. Height 16 feet. Width 9 feet 6 inches.

No. 2.—Constantine contemplating the flaming cross in the sky.

> Signed IAC. D. RIV. Cartoon painted by Romanelli. Height 16 feet. Width 11 feet 3 inches.

No. 3.—Constantine destroying idols and replacing them with Christian statues.

> Signed IAC. D. L. RIV. Cartoon painted by Cortona and still preserved in the Barberini Palace. Height 15 feet 10 inches. Width 12 feet 2 inches.

No. 4.—Naval battle between the fleets of Constantine and Licinius in the Bosphorus.

> Signed IAC. D. L. RIV. Cartoon painted by Charles Neapolitan, pupil of Romanelli, and still preserved in the Barberini Palace. Height 16 feet 4 inches. Length 23 feet.

No. 5.—Constantine burning the Creed of the Arians at Nicæa.

> Signed IAC. D. L. RIV. Cartoon painted by Romanelli and still preserved in the Barberini Palace. Height 15 feet 10 inches. Width 14 feet 10 inches.

No. 6.—Constantine superintending the construction of Constantinople.

> Signed in bottom galon and in right-hand galon. Cartoon painted by Rubens. Height 15 feet 10 inches. Width 15 feet 7 inches.

History of Subjects.

Constantine the Great was born about 274 A.D. and was the first Christian emperor of Rome. His majestic presence, personal courage and commanding abilities made him the idol of the army, and a dangerous rival to the reigning emperors, long before his accession to the purple. In early manhood he followed the example of many other Roman nobles and several Emperors, who fought with wild beasts and gladiators in the amphitheatres before thousands of applauding spectators.

He married the daughter of the Emperor Maximian, about 307 A.D., but soon became embroiled in a war with his august father-in-law, which ended in the latter's defeat and death. There were six Emperors of the Roman world at this era, but Constantine determined to reign supreme and alone. In 312 A.D. he fought a great battle near Rome with the Emperor Maxentius, in which this rival was overwhelmed and slain. He then entered the Eternal City, disbanded the Praetorian guards, destroyed their camp, and assumed the title of " Pontifex Maximus." It was during this war that the traditional miracle occurred, which was the reputed cause of his conversion to Christianity. A flaming cross appeared to his inspired vision, in the sky at noonday, which, according to Eusebius, bore the motto, " In hoc signo vinces," i.e., " By this sign thou shalt conquer." In conspicuous obedience to the imputed command of God, he then embraced Christianity, announced his conversion to his troops, exhibited them the Labarum, declared that this prophetic standard created him vicegerent of God on earth, and predicted that under it he would lead them to continuous victories.

Some authorities assume that he never became a Christian at heart, and insist that the legendary conversion was acknowledged solely to convince his soldiers that his arms would thenceforth be invincible. Although they may question whether he was sincere or not, since he made no effort to suppress pagan worship, yet it is certain that he favored the Christians openly, personally aided in the destruction of idols and other emblems of the heathen deities, and recognized the Christian religion as that of the state.

In 323 A.D. he routed near Adrianople, the Emperor Licinius, who was then the sole survivor of the several Emperors, who originally divided the sovereignty of the Roman world with him. He personally laid siege to Byzantium, and ordered his eldest son, Crispus, to force the Hellespont. The latter, after a terrible naval struggle which lasted two days, defeated Amandus the Admiral of Licinius. Byzantium surrendered, Constantine crossed into Asia, destroyed the army of his rival at Scutari, put him to death, and at last ruled the Roman Empire alone. He securely established his power and authority by wise and enlightened kingcraft, and passed the remainder of his reign in undisturbed tranquility.

In 325 A. D. he convoked the celebrated religious council at Nicæa, as he declared, " to establish throughout his dominions some one definite and complete form of religious worship," and presided at the first meeting. About 300 Bishops assembled, who, after prolonged, acrimonious, and violent discussions, settled upon a creed which stands to this day, as the only " Catholic " or ecumenical one ever discussed and adopted by the representatives of the universal Church. The Arian party made a bold defense of their opinions, and unsuccessfully endeavored to submit and impose their draft of a creed upon the council, but it was torn into pieces and burned.

In 328 A. D., he transferred his court to Byzantium, made that city the capital of the Roman Empire, and changed its name to Constantinople. He gave much personal attention, during several subsequent years, to enlarging, beautifying, and fortifying his beloved city, and died in 337 A. D., dividing the sovereignty of the Roman world between his three sons.

Origin, History and Importance of the Series.

Five of these tapestries issued from the ateliers established in Rome by Cardinal François Barberini under the ægis of his uncle, Pope Urban VIII, and one was woven in the Gobelins during the reign of Louis XIII of France. The Cardinal was for some years Papal Legate at the French Court, and during that period became so enraptured with the magnificent tapestries which decorated the Palaces of her Monarch, with those which King Louis XIII presented him, and with those which he bought personally, that upon his return to Rome he founded in that city a manufactory of them, in order that the Barberini Palace and the Vatican might also be liberally adorned with them. He appointed Jacques de la Riviere, Superintendent, and Jean François Romanelli, Purveyor of cartoons. They began work about the year 1633, were compelled to close the establishment upon the death of Pope Urban

VIII and the banishment of his nephews, and were unable to re-open it until about the year 1660. Five of the tapestries in this series were woven therein before the banishment of the founder, and bear the signature of Jacques de la Riviere. Two of the cartoons were certainly painted by Romanelli, one by Rubens, one by Cortona, one by Neapolitan, and the authorship of the remaining one is attributed by some to Romanelli and by others to Cortona. The writer has examined all three of the cartoons, which are now in the Barberini Palace, and has written biographical sketches of de la Riviere and Romanelli for the purpose of demonstrating, among other things, the artistic and historic importance of the tapestries woven under them in the Barberini Ateliers.

In order to prove the high position in the art world occupied by the sixth tapestry in this series, he inserts the following statements. On page 249 of *"La Tapisserie"* by Eugene Muntz, there is an illustration of a tapestry representing one of the battles of Constantine, which was woven about the beginning of the seventeenth century after a cartoon by Rubens, and is now preserved in the Garde-Meuble in Paris.

In the *" Histoire de la tappisserie depuis le moyen age jusqu'a nos jours "* by Jules Guiffrey, it is declared on page 297, that the cartoons for the History of Constantine by Rubens were interpreted into tapestries at the first manufactory of the Gobelins; on page 301, that parts of two series, woven under de la Planche and de Comans, were inventoried in 1663 amongst the royal tapestries belonging to Louis XIV; and on page 327 that all three suites rank with the series Artemisia in importance and are more val-

uable artistically than the history of Vulcan, a celebrated
production of the Mortlake Atelier.

In the "*Histoire de la Tapisserie en France*" by Jules
Guiffrey, there is an illustration representing the same
battle of Constantine that is represented as heretofore
mentioned in Eugene Müntz's "*La Tapisserie.*"

Among the heliogravure reproductions of the best of
the decorative tapestries in the Garde-Meuble at Paris, as
selected by Guiffard, there is one representing "The
Labarum" after Rubens. This tapestry, as its title indicates, belongs to the series Constantine. Its border is
exactly like that of the sixth tapestry of the series which
is the subject of this monograph, with the exception that
the lateral cartouches in the last named enclose the arms of
France and Navarre, and in the first named the monogram
of de Comans, who was associated with de la Planche in
the superintendency of the first manufactory of the Gobelins.

On page 298 of "*Inventaire du Mobilier de la Cou-
ronne sous Louis XIV*," by Jules Guiffrey, there is the
following description, translated by the writer, of four tapestries belonging to the series Constantine now in the
Garde-Meuble in Paris : "Series of tapestries of silk and
wool relieved in gold, woven in Paris in the manufactory
of the Gobelins, representing the History of Constantine,
after the designs of Rubens, encompassed by a border in
the four corners of which are heads enclosed in cartouches,
at the top a monogram composed of a P and an X
crossed, ⊣ * * and in the bottom an eagle which carries away an serpent."

The writer has examined, by the kind assistance of
Mr. Williamson, Conservateur of the National Garde-

Meuble, almost all the tapestries belonging to the French government which interpret episodes in the life of Constantine the Great, and the results of this examination, joined with the quotations from the works of Guiffrey, and the comparison of the illustration of the sixth tapestry of this series with the illustrations of those heretofore designated, convince him that it was woven in the first manufactory of the Gobelins by de la Planche or de Comans after a cartoon by Rubens.

On pages 72 to 77 of the MSS. XLVIII in Vol. 141, preserved in the Barberini Library, there is, among other things, the following statement, which the Chevalier Zenuti of Florence copied for the writer, and of which the latter inserts below a verbatim translation :

" Account given by the learned Luca Holstenio of the Barberini tapestries with prices, commencing with those which include the history of Constantine the Great, Artemesia, Rinaldo, Diana, etc., presented by the most Christian King, Louis XIII of France, to Cardinal Barberini, Legate to France, 1625."

Holstenio records further on in the same MSS. the titles of all seven of the pieces included in the series Constantine the Great, presented the Cardinal by the King, as above mentioned, and among them appears that of the sixth piece described in this paper, which proves that it is entitled to rank with the most historically important tapestries in existence. He also names the subjects of the five pieces belonging to the same series, which issued as heretofore stated from the Barberini Ateliers, and which were woven by order of the Cardinal more thoroughly to illustrate the history of Constantine the Great. He was not happy, however, in the titles he gave the last named, as he incorrectly read the subjects of most of them.

Eugene Muntz, Conservateur of the Library and Archives in the Beaux Arts at Paris, and the author of several standard works on tapestry, published in 1874 copious extracts from the aforesaid MSS. in the "*Revue des Savantes Savantes*," 5th Series, Vol. VII, pp. 504 to 520, and stated in his preface that in addition to those he copied there extras in the Barberini Library "other documents which contain the description of the Gobelins given Cardinal Barberini by Louis XIII and the Gobelins on sale which were offered him." It was from these "other documents" that the Chevalier Zenuti made the extract hereinbefore translated and introduced.

All the tapestries composing the series described in this paper are enriched with gold and silver threads, and were bought in the Barberini Palace without the assistance of any intermediary. They are absolutely virgin specimens of antique textile art, have not had their colors touched up nor renewed in any fashion, have not been submitted to any alteration nor cutting whatever, and are consequently in all respects, excepting some trifling repairs, exactly in their original condition, as delivered from the Papal Ateliers of Urban VIII and the Royal Ateliers of Louis XIII.

It is but just that these unusual and important advantages should be noted, because so many of the tapestries offered for sale in Europe have been darned or patched instead of repaired after the manner they were originally woven, or their colors have been renovated by the application of paint, or their original borders have been removed and replaced by modern ones far less ornate in design and far more ordinary in execution.

The consent of the Italian Government to the exportation of the celebrated Barberini tapestries was obtained by the powerful friends and connections of the Princesses Barberini, and could not have been secured by any foreigner. The experts chosen by the Italian Minister of Public Instruction declared every tapestry in the collection to be an antique work of art. Consequently the tax of twenty per cent ad valorem which is levied by the Italian Government on all antique works of art it allows to leave Rome, had to be paid on all of them. It was also necessary to have the official seal of the Minister above mentioned affixed to every one in proof of this payment and of the permission to export them. If shipped without these seals they would have been stopped at the frontier by the Custom House authorities, not allowed to leave Italy, and the interested parties would have been subjected to fine and imprisonment.

All the principal newspapers of the kingdom published an account of their sale, several bewailed the nation's loss in sorrowful and indignant language, and some demanded that the Government should reprimand and dismiss the officials who had permitted their exportation. The excitement caused by these publications, and by the speech of Prince Odescalchi in the Italian Senate, censuring the Minister of Public Instruction, decided the purchaser to submit them for increased safety to the National experts of the Royal Galleries of the Uffizi at Florence, who agreed, upon the payment of an additional tax of one per cent ad valorem, to identify them as having already paid the export tax heretofore mentioned, and to attach the seal of said galleries to every one in confirmation of such identification and payment. Consequently each tapestry bears two seals.

To sum up they all possess great historic value, since they have belonged for about 250 years to the Barberini or Rome; they all rank high artistically since they were woven by eminent master-weavers after cartoons by celebrated artists, and were rated as antique objects of art, subject to export tax. None of them have ever been mutilated in any way, and all are among the most important and valuable XVI and XVII century tapestries in existence.

Description of the Borders.

In the centre of the top border of all six of these tapestries is a rose cartouch, which encloses a medallion of flowers encircling the letters PX in gold. In the same position in all the bottom borders is a similarly shaded cartouch which encloses, in five, two branches of laurel upon a gold ground, and in the sixth, an eagle with spreading wings carrying a serpent in its beak.

To the right and left of the central decorations, in the top borders, are bunches of palm sprigs and flowers, and beautiful cornucopias of fruits, flowers, and leaves, all gracefully intertwined with blue scarfs having knotted and tasseled ends. No side borders were ever woven on the first tapestry, and its top border and that of the fifth, are enriched, in excess of the others, with the busts of sphinxes. In each of the four corners, of five, is a polychrome cartouch, two of which enclose heads of men, and two, heads of women, the latter with serpents twined about them. There is also a polychrome cartouch in the centre of all the lateral borders, which encloses an escutcheon emblazoned in eight of said borders, with a golden Barberini bee upon a blue ground, encircled by two sprigs of laurel, and in two of said borders, with the fleur-de-lis of France on the sinister side and with the arms of Navarre on the dexter, both encircled by the collar of the royal French order of the Holy Spirit, with its pendant cross. The Princely crown of the Barberini rests upon the top of each of the lateral cartouches in four of the tapestries, and the Royal crown of France upon each of those in one. From the centre of all of these crowns spring two palm branches, tied with blue ribbons, enveloping a bouquet of flowers which is suspended by ribbons from the decoration in the upper corners. Beneath these cartouches hang, tied together by blue ribbons and interwoven with gold and silver threads, a bouquet of flowers, two palm branches and two trumpets. The dark background throws out in highly artistic relief all the previously mentioned decorations. These borders are not as rich nor as beautiful as some others in the Barberini collection, but they rank amongst the most important historically because they bear the crown and arms of the Barberini family and those of Royal France and Navarre.

The crossed letters PX signify "Pax Christi," and appear on many of the tombs of the ancient martyrs in the catacombs at Rome. The first letter in the Greek word for Christ is X, consequently Christmas is often written Xmas, and " Peace in Christ " PX with the letters superimposed on each other.

Description and Prominent Artistic Merits of Each Tapestry.

The first one never had any lateral borders, having been woven originally for a narrow space like that between two windows. It represents Constantine slaying a lion in single combat, by plunging his sword through its mouth and neck, in an arena before the eyes of some excited soldiers. His figure is the embodiment of courage, power and energy, and his costume is richly laden with gold and silver threads. Although it is evident he realizes the perilous encounter demands all his skill and strength, yet his features display the utmost confidence in his own prowess. The lion is magnificent from its stiffened tail to its savage head and jaws, and is certainly a dangerous antagonist with its terrible teeth and claws and powerful limbs ready to spring upon its foe. All the soldiers watching the scene are grouped in front of a fence, and manifest the deepest interest in the spectacle. Every one of their faces is a study. An array of heads like theirs must have been drawn from life, for invention alone could scarcely have attained such excellence. In the background there is an array of tents, spears and standards of the different cohorts.

Although there is evidence of importance that the cartoon for this tapestry was painted by Romanelli, yet the writer is unable to regard it as conclusive. He questions it because he finds that the character, style and drawing of this tapestry vary materially from some in the Barberini

collection which are, unquestionably, after cartoons by
Romanelli, and from those frescoes in the Louvre at Paris
which are undoubtedly by his hand.   Compare the head of
Constantine in this piece with the heads of the same
Monarch after Romanelli in those representing the Vision
of the Cross in the sky, and the Emperor burning the
Creed of the Arians, and you will doubt the same artist
originated all three of them.   Compare it with the one
after Cortona in the tapestry representing Constantine destroying idols, and you will recognize the same hand probably painted both of them, although the body of the Emperor bears a strong resemblance to some of Romanelli's
productions.   Compare the faces of the excited soldiers
with some of the well known works by Cortona, and you
will believe that he painted the cartoon for them.   In
addition Romanelli preferred classical to gladiatorial subjects, religious fervor to martial frenzy, and mental graces
to physical prowess.

The second tapestry represents Constantine, crowned
with a laurel wreath, standing upon an elevated platform
and contemplating the refulgent cross in gold which blazes
in the sky and which is evidently invisible to the soldiers
about him, since they are completely absorbed in his words
and actions and show neither excitement nor alarm.   Both
loyalty and devotion are strongly imprinted upon their features, which are unfortunately somewhat faded by the
ravages of time.   The face of Constantine is positively
beautiful, and wears an inspired expression as he gazes far
beyond the soldiers grouped around him and apparently
peers into futurity.   His superb costume is richly interwoven with gold and silver threads, but scarcely excels in

magnificence that of the officer in the foreground. All
four of the heads in full view are capitally interpreted.
The cross looks as if woven entirely in gold, and its brilliant rays illuminate the sky in all directions.

The third tapestry represents Constantine, crowned
with laurel, replacing a dethroned idol, in a heathen
temple, with the statue of a Christian prelate. It is
doubtful if Cortona ever produced any heads in oils, and
he created many wonderful paintings, which excel in artistic excellence that of the great Emperor in this tapestry
and those of the two priests in his suite. The Monarch
is also attended by an acolyte bearing a huge cross, and by
two servitors who carefully place, under his guidance, the
image of a Catholic prelate offering benediction, upon the
pedestal from which a pagan deity has been deposed.
Constantine shows his derision of the power ascribed to
idols by placing his foot upon a piece of the one lying
broken upon the floor. The admirable architecture, the
graceful lamps, the toiling servitors, the remarkable features of Constantine and the priests who attend him,
their well proportioned figures, their magnificent costumes
richly interwoven with gold and silver threads, and the
idealistic interpretation of the composition, combine to
render this one of the most important tapestries in the
Barberini collection.

The fourth tapestry represents the celebrated naval
battle in the Bosphorus between the fleets of Constantine,
under the command of his son Crispus, and that of
Licinius, under Admiral Amandus. All the standards of
Constantine are crowned with the cross. The prows of
the ships are decorated with the heads of wild beasts, those

of Constantine with heads of boars, and those of Licinius with heads of lions. Both Crispus and Amandus display the eagle because both are in command of Roman soldiers fighting for the supremacy of their respective Emperors. It is a powerful illustration of a terrific struggle, and clearly portrays the sublime courage of the ancient Romans, no matter in what perilous positions the fortunes of war placed them. In proof of which examine the features of the three men who have quit a sinking ship and boldly swim towards their adversaries upon an uninjured one. They realize they are dreadfully overmatched by those awaiting them, but they do not hesitate to accept the risks of fighting under such fearful odds. Every face is a masterpiece in which one can clearly read the emotions which animate its owner. The Admiral has given up the struggle, as the despair in his features and in his gestures amply testifies. All the soldiers are superb specimens of fighting material, strong, athletic, well proportioned and full of vigor. Their terrible contest has been so ably interpreted that we almost hear the clang of their arms and their hoarse shouts of victory and defiance.

Every part has been well conceived and developed, beginning with the superb costumes of gold and silver threads, taking in turn the agitated water, the rolling smoke, the rising, falling or sinking ships, and ending with the drowning and fighting warriors. It is a magnificent tapestry, a chef d'œuvre of Roman textile art worthy of a prominent place in any museum in the world.

The fifth tapestry represents Constantine burning the Creed of the Arians at Nicæa. He thrusts it into a fire glowing upon a brazier held by a kneeling servitor. He is crowned with laurel, and wears a mantle, richly decorated with gold, over a costume interwoven with silver. His figure is majestic, but his pensive face lacks strength. All the other personages are powerfully drawn and their costumes are heavily charged with gold and silver threads. Their faces are mirrors, and with their gestures clearly portray the emotions controlling them. Cynical humility, constrained anger, rapt devotion, gratified ambition, devout thankfulness, and calm contentment, can be read on their countenances in the above order, beginning with the cowled monk and sweeping round the foreground to the Prelate next the Emperor. The marbles in the architectural background have been beautifully reproduced, and the colors in the costumes skilfully harmonized. The whole tapestry would rank as a masterpiece if Constantine's face had more character and if the flesh tints of all the personages had not lost much more from the ravages of time than the deeper and stronger colors of their eyes and their robes.

The sixth tapestry represents Constantine superintending the construction of Constantinople. He is crowned with laurel and wears an imperial mantle interwoven with gold and silver threads. A magnificent eagle rides the air above him, holding a laurel wreath in its beak and claws, which symbolizes that Fortune, in the guise of the principal emblem of Jupiter, continually hovers over her favorite son, and is always ready to crown him with the garland of victory. Behind him stands one of his suite, an attentive observer of the scene, and in front, the kneeling architect points out with a pair of compasses, on a plan held up to their view by a servitor, the proposed additions to the city. Constantine indicates, by the movement of his hand, the quarter of the town in which certain work shall be done, and the architect, by pointing in the same direction, signifies that he understands his monarch's instructions. To the left a sculptor chisels the decoration on a column, and further off two men pry and move certain completed pieces of architecture. In the background is an exquisite glimpse of Byzantium, the sea of Marmora, and the hills along the Bosphorus. It is a powerful, well grouped composition. The four most important personages have remarkable heads and figures, but the artists have excelled themselves in the majestic pose, clear cut features, thoughtful eyes, and rich costume of Constantine. The grand head of the kneeling architect is evidently a portrait, for the eyes, beard, beetling brows, and earnest face have been reproduced with such signal success that they must have been taken from life. All the colors are well preserved, even the flesh tints have almost retained their original strength. It is, in conclusion, a museum tapestry and ranks among the most celebrated of the era of Louis XIII, as would be expected from the renowned abilities of the artist who painted the cartoon, and the illustrious reputation of the establishment in which it was woven.

The Series Chateau and Garden Scenes.

Composed of Four Tapestries.

No. 7.—Arbor in three sections, supported on eight caryatides.
>   Height 15 feet. Width 13 feet 10 inches.

No. 8.—Arbor in part of three sections, supported on four caryatides.
>   Height 15 feet. Width 14 feet 2 inches.

No. 9.—Arbor in one section, supported on four caryatides.
>   Height 15 feet. Width 11 feet 4 inches.

No. 10.—Arbor in one section, supported on eight caryatides.
>   Height 15 feet. Width 12 feet 8 inches.

These tapestries formerly belonged to Cardinal Antoine Barberini, Grand Prior of France, who resided during the latter part of his life in Paris and died there. On the settlement of his estate they were sent to Rome and incorporated in the collection of his family in the Barberini Palace.

Each tapestry represents a chateau in the background, a garden in the center plan, and the families of the proprietors amusing themselves in several ways beneath or near huge arbors in the foreground. The subjects were no doubt inspired by the study of the celebrated series now in the Garde Meuble, at Paris, representing the " Royal Palaces of France," because the compositions are of the same character and are developed upon similar lines, although the motives are vastly different.

It would appear that the third and fourth pieces were woven about the middle of the XVII century in the Faubourg St. Germain at Paris in the atelier of Raphael de la Planche, as they bear his monogram in the dexter upright galon and the initial letter of Paris and the fleur de lis of France in the bottom galon, which are the marks of his atelier.

It is evident that the first and second pieces were woven about the beginning of the XVII century at Brussels in the atelier of Jacques Geubles, as they bear his monogram in the dexter upright galon. It is not easy to satisfactorily account for the difference of origin in the first and last half of this series, although the presumption is that Cardinal Barberini bought the first and second pieces already made, and desiring more of the same style, ordered the third and fourth pieces woven in Paris when he was residing there.

In the center of the top and bottom border is a vase of flowers, upon each side of which are festoons of leaves, flowers and fruits, reaching from the center to the corners and attached at both ends by reddish colored ribbons. The motive in each bottom corner is a vase of flowers and leaves, and that in each top corner a pendant bouquet of fruits and leaves. The principal motives of the lateral borders are three bouquet holders of architectural designs, from each of which springs a bouquet or falls a cascade of leaves, flowers and fruits.   The general tone of the whole series is delicious, soft and harmonious.

In the first tapestry (No. 7) the arbor filling the whole upper plan is divided into three sections supported by eight caryatides, six of which are female and two male, all standing upon pedestals.   The central opening is rounded at the top and the other two form straight arches, the summits of all being crowned by vases of flowers.   There are also vases of flowers standing at the points where these archways intersect each other, and where they join the border. The whole central plan is occupied by a moderate-sized chateau and a tremendous garden laid out in French style, ornamented with a handsome fountain and partly surrounded on the upper side by an exceedingly decorative arbored promenade covered with vines.   In the foreground a man and woman sit upon a sofa placed beneath the central arch.   He plays upon an old-fashioned guitar or mandolin and she listens attentively, although the dog in her lap apparently howls at the music.   A second couple approach through the sinister opening walking arm in arm, and a hunter with falcon upon his wrist, game-bag at his side, and accompanied by two dogs, approaches through the dexter.   In the extreme front there is a peacock and hen. Landscape background dotted with buildings and terminating in mountains.   The personages are mainly Flamands but the musical couple are strikingly English in style and wear costumes of the era of Elizabeth of England, as is particularly manifest in the high ruffled collar of the woman.

In the second tapestry (No. 8) the arbor filling the whole upper plan is supported by four caryatides, standing upon pedestals, is covered with vines, and has the figure of an eagle in the centre at the top. The background is made up of rolling country, which is covered with clumps of forest or orchards of fruit trees, and terminates in mountains, one of which is crowned by an antique looking building. The central plan is occupied by a magnificent chateau, with a large garden in front and on both sides, which is laid out in French style, with parallel paths, generally separated by rows of hedges supported by fences, and ornamented with a magnificent fountain surmounted with a bronze figure. Three couples promenade in the garden and two women are engaged in watering the plants and flowers. In the foreground a gamekeeper holds a dog in leash, the master and mistress of the chateau walk towards the spectator, and the mistress raises her fan as if to reprimand the lovers seated upon the ground, for " Rinaldo " reclines in the lap of " Armida " and plays with a dog which has placed its forepaws upon his knee. In the immediate foreground are a turkey cock and hen, and a stork. The personages are Flamands, as in the preceding tapestry, but wear costumes more decidedly Flemish in character.

In the third tapestry (No. 9) the arbor spanning the upper plan and which springs from a base supported by four caryatides standing upon pedestals, is covered with grape vines. A huge grape vine twines around each caryatid and a vase of flowers stands upon the capitals of the nearest two of them. The central plan is filled by a marble palace built in the shape of an amphitheatre, and a large garden laid out in French style. Upon the cornice of the palace and in the niches around the courtyard stand a number of marble figures. Upon the stream of water which crosses the

tapestry at the foot of the garden floats a boat with one
tower. Beneath a canopy in the stern of the boat sit a
Lord and Lady, probably the owners of the palace; and in
the bow sits a courtier playing upon an antique musical instrument. On the bank between the stream and the palace
stand a couple of courtiers interested in watching the gamekeeper who has taken a rabbit from the trap in front of
him and presents it to the lady. In the foreground another
courtier, accompanied by a dog, has raised his cross-bow to
shoot a hare which is partly concealed in the grass on the
left. The water in the stream is positively transparent,
and reflects the boat and its passengers, the gentleman and
lady upon the bank, as well as part of the arbor, with surprising naturalness. The personages are evidently Flamands, although some could be mistaken for English and wear
costumes closely approaching the character of those in
vogue during the reign of the great Elizabeth.

In the fourth tapestry (No. 10) the arbor traversing
the upper plan springs from a base supported by eight caryatides standing upon pedestals, instead of four as in the
preceding tapestry, and is covered by the vines of the lemon
instead of the grape. In the background is a fine old palace
from which a broad path stretches, with an evergreen wall
upon both sides, through a large French garden, to the
beautiful fountain overflowing with water near the foreground. Upon this path walks a gardener carrying his
tools and a courtier approaching the group in the first plan.
The garden contains a couple of small fountains and several evergreen arches, like those in the gardens at Versailles,
through one of which appear the figures of a man and
woman. To the right of the large fountain stand two

women who seem to be amused at the misfortunes of their
sister on its left, who has become entangled in the iron net-
work surrounding it and from which a courtier endeavors
to disentangle her. In the foreground another courtier
kneeling, is evidently playing a game something like our
ring-toss. Near him stands a gardener with uncovered head
who leans upon the pedestal of a caryatid and gazes intently towards the couple upon the opposite side of the
fountain. In the right foreground are a couple of dogs at
play. It may be that the whole scene in the first plan
illustrates an ancient game. Both the courtiers are fine
looking men, very picturesquely costumed, and are evidently Flamands, although the tapestry was woven in Paris, and
although their costumes are scarcely pure Flemish.

The Series Events in the Life of Moses.

Composed of 6 tapestries, only one of which is exhibited because the others have not yet arrived from Europe.

No. 11. Moses and his wife Zipporah taking care of the lambs of his father in law Jethro's flock.

These tapestries were woven in Brussels, Brabant, during the second half of the XVI century and are as superb examples of Flemish art at its apogee as can be found in any European Museum.

The figures are colossal, are remarkable for their grandeur, nobility and seriousness, as well as for their life and movement.

This tapestry was woven in comparatively few colors, all of which have grown softer and lovelier by the toning effects of over three centuries. The shades of color have been hatched with consummate skill, and the whole technical execution has never been surpassed in any age. The costumes are rich as well as picturesque. The borders are practically perfect examples of textile painting. It is evident that the artist-weaver fairly revelled in exhibiting the greatly varied and marvellous beauties that can be portrayed in warp and woof. Every separate motive possesses original and individual charms and the grace and skill with which they have been combined proves that the weaver was not only master of all the mysteries and traditions of his own art but was a poet who could write in tissue.

36

Monograph Series Judith and Holofernes.

Composed of Eight Tapestries.

History of the Subjects.

The following history of Judith and Holofernes has been mainly compiled from the " Book of Judith " as printed in the earlier editions of the Old Testament.

According to this record, Judith was a beautiful Jewish widow and throughout all her life was a model of piety, courage, and chastity.

Holofernes was a savage instrument of the King of Assyria, who carried war, desolation and famine throughout a large extent of God's territory.

Nebuchadnezzar, King of Nineveh (Assyria), sent envoys to "all the inhabitants of the land" commanding them to join his standards in his war against Arphaxad. The Assyrian Monarch was unknown to several of the nations which received his peremptory order, and therefore they laughed at his mandate and treated his embassadors with contempt. Nebuchadnezzar, enraged at their contumeliousness, " swore by his throne and his kingdom, that he would avenge himself by destroying all flesh that did not obey the commandment of his mouth." To this end he summoned his officers and his nobles to whom he communicated his determination, which they unanimously supported. When this council was ended, he called into his presence Holofernes, the chief captain of his army, who knelt before him and above whom he extended his sceptre, as it was a law amongst the Persians and Assyrians that every one summoned into the royal presence, and over

39

whom the Monarch did not extend his sceptre, should be put to death. The omission of the King to do this, whether intentional or accidental, was equivalent to a condemnation of the unfortunate subject.

The sealed orders which Nebuchadnezzar delivered to Holofernes began with the words, "Thus saith the great King, the Lord of the whole earth," and after commanding him to ravage and lay waste the lands of those who resisted, and destroy the inhabitants thereof, the monarch terminated with the threat, "and take thou heed, that thou transgress none of the commandments of thy Lord."

Holofernes carried out these terrible commands with savage ferocity. As he approached Judea, dealing death and destruction everywhere, he issued the decree that he came "to destroy all the gods of the land, and that all nations should worship Nebuchadnezzar only, and that all tongues and tribes should call upon him as God." The children of Israel "were troubled, for Jerusalem and for the temple of the Lord their God," when they heard of this decree, and the fate of those who resisted it, but they courageously gathered together their warriors to fortify their villages and to guard the narrow passes into the valleys of Judea. Their resistance excited Holofernes to frenzy. He summoned the "princes of Moab and the captains of Ammon" and demanded, "Who are these people, what is the multitude of their army, wherein is their power and strength, what king is set over them, or who is captain of their army?" Achior stepped forward to enlighten him, and recited the history of the Jews, traced their wanderings with his finger upon a map, declared that "if there be error in this people and they sin against their God, we shall over-

come them, but if there be no iniquity in their nation," he
advised Holofernes to pass them by " lest their Lord defend
them, and we become a reproach before all the world."

When Achior had finished, Holofernes, flaming with
passion, demanded, " Who art thou, Achior, who darest
prophesy that we should not make war against Israel
because their God will defend them, and who is God but
Nebuchadnezzar?" He then ordered that Achior should
be immediately seized, bound and delivered to the Jews,
and thus perish with the people he presumed invincible, for
Holofernes had doomed them to destruction.

The next day Holofernes surrounded Bethulia, the
first fortified city of the Jews, and took possession of the
fountains and wells upon which the people depended for
water. At the expiration of thirty-four days, the beleaguered citizens, having exhausted their cisterns, assembled and demanded that their chief, Ozias, should sur-
render the city to Holofernes. Ozias bade them keep up
their courage for five days longer, and if then no help came
from the Lord he would accede to their prayers. When
Judith heard of the demands of the people and the reply of
Ozias, she sent for him and " Chabris and Charmis, the
ancients of the city," and said: " O ye governors of
Bethulia, the words ye have spoken before the people this
day are not right, wherein you have promised to deliver the
city to our enemies in five days, unless within these days
the Lord turn to help us. Nay, my brethren, provoke not
the Lord our God to anger. For if He will not help us
within these five days, He hath power to defend us when
He will, even every day, or to destroy us before our
enemies. Do not bind the counsels of the Lord our God,

for God is not as man, that he may be threatened, neither is he as the son of man that he should be wavering. Therefore, let us wait for salvation of him, and call upon him to help us, and he will hear our voice if it please him." And then she asked, "Who are ye that have threatened God this day?" She arraigned them in forcible language and methaphorically showed them that their vanity, enviousness, obstinacy, self-sufficiency and cupidity, outweighed in the scales their honor, their reliance upon the justice of God, their hope in him, and their faith in their religion. Continuing she said: "For if we be taken, so all Judea shall lie waste, and our sanctuary shall be spoiled, and he will require the profanation thereof at our mouth. And the slaughter of our brethren and the captivity of the country and the desolation of our inheritance will he turn upon our heads among the Gentiles, wheresoever we shall be in bondage, and we shall be an offence and a reproach to all them that possess us. For our servitude shall not be directed to favor, but the Lord our God shall turn it to dishonor. Now, therefore, O brethren! let us show an exemple to our brethren, because their hearts depend upon us, and the sanctuary and the house and the altar rest upon us. Moreover, let us give thanks to the Lord our God, which trieth us, even as he did our fathers. For he hath not tried us in the fire as he did them, for the examination of their hearts, neither hath he taken vengeance on us, but the Lord doth scourge them that come near unto him, to admonish him."

Ozias, Chabris and Charmis replied, " there is none to gainsay thy wisdom, all the people know thy understanding, but the oath we have taken we will not break, therefore

pray thou that the Lord will send rain to fill our cisterns."
To which Judith answered, " I will do a thing which shall
go throughout all generations to the children of our nation,
stand ye by the gates this night and I will go forth with my
waiting-woman, and within the five days the Lord will
visit Israel by my hand, but I will not declare it unto you."
Ozias and the princes respond " Go in peace, and the Lord
God be before thee and take vengeance on our enemies."
With this they departed and Judith most supplicatingly ap-
pealed in prayer to the Lord, against the Assyrians " to give
into mine hand the power that I have conceived, smite by
the deceit of my lips their prince and break down their
stateliness by the hand of a woman."

She then entered her house and called her maids, who
removed " the garments of her widowhood ; anointed her
with precious ointment ; braided her hair ; put a tire upon
her head; and clothed her in her garments of gladness. They
put sandals upon her feet, and decked her with bracelets,
chains, rings, earrings, and all her ornaments to allure the
eyes of all men that should see her." Then she gave her
maid a bag of provisions, and they went forth from the
gate of the city towards the camp of Holofernes. As
they approached, they were halted by the guard, who inquired " Of what people art thou ?" and she answered, " I
am a woman of the Hebrews and am fled from them, for
they shall be given you to be consumed ; I am come to
show your Chief Captain a way whereby he shall win all
the hill country around Bethulia, without losing any of his
men." With that the guard conducted her to the tent of
Holofernes who " rested upon his bed under a canopy,
which was woven with purple, and gold, and emeralds, and

precious stones," and when Judith came before him, " she fell upon her knees and did reverence unto him and his guards lifted her up."

Holofernes inquired of her " wherefore hast thou fled from thy people and hast come to us, none shall hurt thee, but entreat thee well," to which Judith answered, " if thou wilt follow the words of thy handmaid, God will deliver Israel into thy hands. Achior repeated to us the words which he declared unto thee, and I entreat thee reject not his advice for it is true; but the people have naught to eat nor drink, and they will lay hands upon their cattle and on all those sanctified things that God hath forbidden them to touch or to eat. I, thy handmaid, knowing all this, am fled and God hath sent me to advise thee. Now therefore, my Lord, I will remain with thee, and thy servant will go out by night into the valley and pray unto my God and he will tell me when they have committed these sins and the same day thou shalt destroy them." Her words pleased Holofernes and he marvelled at her beauty and her wisdom. He declared that " if thou do as thou has spoken, thou shalt dwell in the house of King Nebuchadnezzar, and shalt be renowned through the whole earth," and desired that " she should eat of his meats and drink of his wines," but Judith replied, " provision shall be made for me of the things that I have brought, lest I commit an offense." The guard then conducted her to a tent and about the morning watch she sent to Holofernes, saying, " let my Lord now command that thine handmaid may go forth unto prayer." Holofernes " commanded his guard that they should not stay her," and thus for three nights she went out and in un-molested. On the fourth day Holofernes " made a feast to his servants only, and called none of the officers to the banquet " and sent Bagoas, the eunuch, " to persuade the Hebrew woman to eat and drink with us."

Judith consented, and when she appeared " Holofernes was enthralled and only awaited a time to deceive her." He begged that she should " drink now and be merry with us," but Judith " ate and drank before him only what her maid had prepared. Holofernes took great delight in her, and drank much more wine than he had drank at any time in one day since he was born." The feast was long and the servants were weary, so " Bagoas dismissed them, shut the tent without, and went to his bed. Judith was left alone in the tent, and Holofernes lying upon his bed for he was filled with wine. Now Judith had commanded her maid to stand without her bedchamber as she did daily, for she had said to Bagoas that she would go forth to her prayers," as usual.

Alone with the oppressor of her race and kindred; alone with the savage who had desolated whole countries and filled nations with mourning, and that savage in her power—asleep and drunken—Judith hesitated but a moment, then seized the falchion of Holofernes, took hold of his hair, and with two strokes severed his head from his body. She handed the head to her maid, who put it into the bag which held their provisions, " so the twain went forth together according to their custom unto prayer " outside the camp, and proceeded straightway to Bethulia, before whose gates Judith cried out " Open, open now the gate : praise God, praise God, for He hath not taken away His mercy from the house of Israel, but hath destroyed our enemies by mine hands this night." They opened the

gates for her, and when she had entered and mounted the
steps of the temple " she took the head out of the bag and
showed it and said unto them, Behold the head of Holofernes, the Chief Captain of the army of Assur, the Lord
hath smitten him by the hand of a woman.   Then all the
people were wonderfully astonished," and sang and danced
and played on timbrels, and with glad music praised the
Lord.

Ozias with uplifted hand cried, " O daughter, blessed
art thou of the most high God above all the women upon
earth."   Judith then sent for Achior " that he may see and
know the head of him that despised the house of Israel,
and that sent him (Achior) to us, as it were to his death."
When Achior came and saw and heard, he fell upon his
knees and reverenced Judith and was converted to Judaism.

Judith then said, " take this head and hang it upon the
highest place of your walls, and take ye every one his
weapons and go forth out of the City as though ye would go
down into the field toward the watch of the Assyrians;
but go not down."   Upon seeing you " they shall go into
their camp and raise up the Captain of the army of Assur,
and they shall run to the tent of Holofernes, but shall not
find him; then fear shall fall upon them, and they shall
flee before your face."

The warriors followed the advice of Judith, the Assyrians did as she had prophesied, the Israelites pursued them
with fearful slaughter, and the immense riches of the army
of Holofernes fell into the hands of the Jews.   They
gave to Judith " the tent of Holofernes, all his plate and
vessels of gold, and all his rich stuffs and precious stones,
and all his treasures."

List of the Tapestries composing this series, with the Latin inscription in the top border of each, a Translation thereof, and the size of each Tapestry with its signature.

Inscription.

No. 12.—NABVCHODONOSOR REX HOLOFERNEM PRINCIPEM MILITIÆ SVÆ ADVERSVS ISRAELEM MITTIT.

TRANSLATION.—King Nebuchadnezzar sends Holofernes, the chief captain of his army, against Israel. Signed E. Leyniers.
Height 13 feet. Width 11 feet 7 inches.

Inscription.

No. 13.—ACHIOR, DVX AMONITARV ENARRANS DEI ISRAELIS POTENTIAM IVSSV HOLOFERNIS CAPITVR.

TRANSLATION. Achior, the leader of the Ammonites while expounding the power of the God of Israel, is arrested by order of Holofernes. Signed H. Rydams.
Height 13 feet 3 inches. Width 13 feet 4 inches.

Inscription.

No. 14.—IVDITH VIDVA PONDERAT POPVLI VIRTVTES ET VITIA HIS SVPERANTIBVS ISRAEL PVNITVR;

TRANSLATION.—The widow, Judith, weighed the virtues and the vices of the people; when the latter are the heavier, Israel is punished. Signed H. Rydams.
Height 13 feet 2 inches. Width 15 feet 6 inches. In the heavier scale are the following emblems of vice, each of which has its appropriate significance : A mask, a snake biting a heart, a ram's head, peacock feathers, and a bag of money on which sits a toad. In the lighter scale are the following emblems of virtue, each of which has its appropriate significance : An anchor, a pair of scales, and a sword, a heart emitting fire, a lamb's head, an altar and two clasped hands.

Inscription.

No. 15.—IVDITH PVLCHERRIMA INDVIT SE VESTIBUS IVCVNDITATIS SVÆ VT BETHVLIAM AB EXCIDIO LIBERET.

TRANSLATION.—The most beautiful Judith arrays herself in garments of gladness, in order that she may free Bethulia from destruction. Signed E. Leyniers.
Height 13 feet 2 inches. Width 11 feet 9 inches.

Inscription.

No. 16.—IVDITH FVGITIVA HOLOFERNEM ASTVTE DECIPIT ET SPECIOSAM VICTORIAM PROMITTIT.

TRANSLATION.—Judith in the guise of a fugitive cunningly deceives Holofernes and promises him a specious victory. Signed II. Rydams.
Height 13 feet Width 13 feet 3 inches.

Inscription.

No. 17.—HOLOFERNES EBRIVS A IVDITH CAPITE TRONCATVR QUÆ ITA ISRAELEM SERVAT.

TRANSLATION.—Holofernes, while drunken, is deprived of his head by Judith who thus saves Israel. Signed E. Leyniers.
Height 13 feet 4 inches. Width 14 feet 11 inches.

Inscription.

No. 18.—IVDITH VICTRIX HOLOFERNIS CAPVT POPVLO EXHIBET QVI DEVM ISRAELIS LAVDAT.

TRANSLATION.—Judith – Victress – displays the head of Holofernes to the people who praise the God of Israel. Signed II. Rydams.
Height 13 feet. Width 17 feet 2 inches.

Inscription.

No. 19.—DEVS ISRAELIS EXERCITVM HOLOFERNIS FVNDIT ET MVNERA IVDITH DANTVR.

TRANSLATION.—The God of Israel routes the army of Holofernes, and treasures are given to Judith. Signed E. Leyniers.
Height 13 feet 3 inches. Width 18 feet 10 inches.

Description of Each Tapestry in this Series.

The first tapestry (No. 12) represents Nebuchadnezzar seated upon his throne, and extending his sceptre over the head of Holofernes, who kneels as he receives from the King's hand the edict, which bears the Monarch's portrait on its seal, and which commands him upon forfeit of his life, to kill all those who disobeyed the King's behests, to destroy their towns and cities and lay waste their lands. To the left of the Monarch stand a few of his great officers, to his right are some of lesser degree, and a number of soldiers. Judging by what they present us, it cannot be said that the artists who created this tapestry believed that Nebuchadnezzar, Holofernes, or any of the other magnates were handsome men; on the contrary, they portray to us ferocious, hard and savage looking beings, just such men as would be capable of originating and executing terrible deeds. In this they have been eminently successful, as all the visages clearly indicate what might be expected of their several owners. In all else but their faces, they are superb men, gigantic in stature, strong of limb and magnificently costumed. The artists of the XVII century recoiled from depicting vice as beautiful, or ferocity as handsome featured. Their simpler lives and faiths forbade such monstrosities and it would be far better if the artists and litterateurs of the XIX century returned to those earlier and more wholesome ideas and principles. The background effects of marble in columns, archway and walls, and the draperies over the head of Nebuchadnezzar are all reproduced with wonderful fidelity and skill.

The second tapestry (No. 13) represents Achior, Captain of the Ammonites, standing behind a table in front of a tent, with his left arm uplifted to give greater weight to the words he utters, as he points out upon a map the wanderings of the Jews, recites their history and declares that they cannot be conquered so long as they obey the commandments of their Lord. Holofernes in frenzied fury has turned his back to the table, and with a ferocious look he designates Achior by a gesture and orders the guards to arrest him. One has already seized the Ammonite Chief, and the others press forward to obey the orders of their General. In the background some soldiers are fighting; one cuts loose a prisoner who has been tied to the limbs of a tree, and two fine-looking fellows in the right foreground guard the tent of Holofernes. This is a superb tapestry. The table with its beautiful cover of embroidered cloth, the books and maps and the background scenes, are all well done, but the great abilities of the artists are more prominently displayed in the grand figures of the principal personages, their magnificent costumes or suits of armor, the graceful plumes in their helmets, their doughty spears, and above all in the remarkably appropriate expressions woven into their features.

The third tapestry (No. 14 not here exhibited) represents Judith metaphorically weighing the vices and virtues of the people of Israel. Almost in the centre of the tapestry, there is a huge pair of scales, held up by a hand descending from a cloud. In the lighter scale there are emblems of virtue; while in the heavier scale there are emblems of vice.

Judith stands before the scales and declares that when

this state of things exists amongst the people of Israel, God will surely punish them.

The fourth tapestry (No. 15) represents Judith, assisted by her maids, arraying herself in a bewitching toilet to dazzle and entrap Holofernes. She stands in front of a table near the middle of an exquisitely draped boudoir, and gazes into a mirror. A kneeling maid fastens a bracelet upon her wrist, another spreads a rich mantle over her shoulders, a third takes an additional garment out of a chest, and the fourth, who accompanied Judith to the camp of the Assyrian General, carries a salver and an ewer. On the floor is a brazier containing some curling tongs. Upon the table, which is covered with a handsomely embroidered cloth, stands a jewel chest and the top of the latter is decorated with a vase of flowers. A necklace of pearls hangs from the open drawer of the chest and a collar of similar gems lies upon the table.

The whole composition is not only artistically attractive but biblically interesting. The artists have created a lovely and fervent Judith who, as any one will realize by studying her face, possessed the moral courage to risk her life to save her country from destruction. The maids are excellent, and are serving their mistress with ability, but they play only a secondary part in so far as the interest in the story is concerned. It is a charming tableau admirably interpreted, particularly in the position and drawing of the personages, in the life and movement woven into their figures, and in the soft and harmonious colors of their costumes and those of the furnishings in the room.

The fifth tapestry (No. 16) represents Holofernes seated upon his bed at the entrance to his tent, where he was resting in Oriental luxuriousness, propped round with soft cushions. Judith kneels at his feet, with downcast eyes and clasped hands. The story of her mission is legibly written upon her face and had she exposed it to the gaze of Holofernes, he might readily have read her purpose. The Assyrian Chief leans forward and offers his hand to aid Judith to her feet, and one can clearly read the ferocity of his character upon his features. At the side of the bed are his plumed helmet, his sword and belt and his coat of mail. The two soldiers who have conducted Judith to the tent of Holofernes, assist her to rise at the command of their Chief. Their strong, stolid features are powerfully interpreted, but the artists have shown even greater ability in the consciously cunning look they have given the features of Judith, and the half-deceitful, half-devoted glances woven in the face of her handmaid. The latter kneels behind her mistress and carries the train of her mantle and the bag of provisions they have brought with them.

The composition of the tableau is excellent, all the personages are well drawn, and the details are carefully executed, and the mantle of Judith is magnificent. The closer they copied flesh tints in tissue the greater the disposition to fade. Consequently those in Judith's face have faded, whilst the swarthier skin colors of the others have successfully resisted the corroding effects of time. This fading of the flesh tints wherever it occurs in this series can be readily reproduced, however, by skillfully embroidering in silk threads of the appropriate colors. This will not change nor alter the characte nror appearance her features originally had, but on the contrary it will simply replace the lost shades of color.

The sixth tapestry (No. 17) represents the banquet offered Judith by Holofernes in his tent when camped before Bethulia. The Assyrian Chief holds aloft a huge crystal and bronze goblet of wine and essays to clasp the hand of the lovely Jewess, but with a wistful far-away look in her eyes she takes no heed of the act nor of the enraptured glances with which he insults her. Old Bagoas, bearing his lictor's axe, busies himself in spreading upon the table the viands and fruits handed him by an attendant. A page in the foreground fills an ewer with wine, whilst the handmaid passes to her mistress the food and wine they had brought with them, because Judith refused to eat or drink anything offered her by Holofernes. The table is decorated with a magnificent peacock, placed between two huge candles, and further back we see the casqued head of a soldier. In the background, and visible under the drapery of the tent of Holofernes, there is another banquet scene in an open tent.

This is both a superb as well as pathetic tapestry. The amorous Assyrian, the indifferent Bagoas, the curious soldier and attendant and the occupied boy, all speak to the observer in one direction, whilst the affrighted handmaid, and the serene but earnest look on the face of Judith as she reflects upon her dangerous mission and its possible results, trouble you as would the sight of a lamb in the jaws of a tiger. The tapestry is superb in its light and shade effects, in the rich vessels of gold and bronze, in the draperies, in the table ornaments, in the magnificent costume of Judith and in the wondrously toned colors. It is high art indeed; all the main accessories are splendidly reproduced, and each countenance tells its own tale without need of words. The reader will remark that the artists have happily not represented the actual tragedy as recited in the inscription on the tapestry and on page 45 of this work, but the banquet scene which led up to it.

The seventh tapestry (No. 18, not here exhibited) represents the return of Judith to Bethulia. On the topmost step at the entrance to the temple she holds aloft the head of the ferocious Holofernes. In the background are the towers and walls of the beleaguered city, and between these and the temple the people with shouts of joy praise the Lord for their deliverance.

The eighth tapestry (No. 19, not here exhibited) represents Judith still humble and with the far-away look in her eyes, standing upon a platform outside the walls of Bethulia, surrounded by her maids, the great dignitaries of the city gathered near her on her right, whilst some soldiers appear on her left with Achior at their head.

Description of the Borders of this Series.

In the centre of the top border of every one is a grey cartouch, the upper part of which is decorated with the mask or head of a satyr in yellow, and the lower part with dolphins in the same color. In this cartouch, on a blue background, is a Latin inscription which designates the subject of its respective tapestry. To the right and left of this cartouch, excepting in the narrow tapestries, are standing eagles with extended wings, and festoons of leaves and fruit, which in the wide tapestries are apparently suspended from the decorations which cross the backs of the eagles.

In the centre of the bottom borders of every one is a

yellow cartouch, which encloses, in No. 12 Narcissus attempting to seize the reflection of his own image in a fountain; in No. 13, Perseus on the winged horse Pegasus delivers Andromeda from the sea-monster; in No. 14, Diana and two nymphs going to the chase accompanied by several dogs; in No. 15, Perseus with the head of Medusa; in No. 16, Apollo and metamorposis of Daphne into a laurel tree; in No. 17, practically the same as No. 15; in No. 18, Neptune carrying off Proserpine; and in No. 19, Bellerophon on the winged horse Pegasus, kills the dragon Chimæra. These small figures, with some notable exceptions, are carelessly drawn, inasmuch as they are only humble accessories.

To the right and left of these central cartouches are winged cherubs, and beyond these are cornucopias of fruit and leaves, each of which, in some of the tapestries, is attached by a ribbon to the central and corner cartouches, which ribbons are held up by the winged cherubs mentioned above.

In the four corners of each tapestry are grey cartouches, enclosing the mask or head of a satyr in yellow.

Each of those in the upper corner holds a ring in its mouth, into which are knotted two ribbons, one connecting it to the festoons of leaves and fruit in the top borders, and from the other swings a bunch of fruit and leaves (whilst from each bottom corner cartouch springs a cornucopia of fruits and leaves).

In the centre of each lateral border is a grey cartouch enclosing a mass of color in imitation of a convex mirror, above which is a shell, and beneath which are dolphins, both in yellow.

In conclusion, the borders of this series are remarkable
for the harmony of their details, the softness of their colors
and for their unusually effective association of flowers,
fruits, leaves, figures, etc.

Origin, History and Artistic Value of the Series.

These tapestries were woven in Flanders in the third
quarter XVII century, in an atelier in Brussels, as is
proven by the mark BUB on each one and the signatures
of H. Rydams and E. Leyniers. They are remarkably
decorative and exceedingly fine in quality. The figures of
the principal personages are magnificent and their costumes
superb. As further evidence of their importance and
value, I translate what J. Guiffrey in his " *Histoire de la
tapisserie depuis le moyen age jusqu 'a nos jours* " writes
on pages 272, 275 of the chefs d'atelier, under whom they
were manufactured.

" The Leyniers family ranked with the greatest in
Flanders, both in the number and the ability of the tapestry
artists it produced. The following is a list of the principal
members of this dynasty : Gaspard, a tapestry weaver
who was continually occupied with his many orders, and
who was brother of Daniel Leyniers, of whom mention
has already been made ; Everard, son of Gaspard, born in
1597, and who died in 1680, ' covered with glory,' and who
continued in his career until he had attained his eightieth
year. In a competitive exposition held in 1650 by the
most celebrated tapestry weavers in Flanders, Everard was
awarded the highest medal over all his rivals. [This
Everard Leyniers is the author and signer of one-half of

this series Judith and Holofernes.] Urbain, son of Gaspard, was one of the most celebrated dyers of his time. He preserved and employed the secrets of his father in coloring the wools."

The excellence of his work brought to Gaspard the title of " Dyer to the Governor of the Netherlands," and the exclusive monopoly of dyeing all the wools used in all the ateliers of Brussels, a most important and extraordinary privilege and tribute.

Everard had three sons, John, Daniel and Giles, all of whom followed the career of their father. John, whose reputation eclipsed that of his brothers, executed a series representing the History of Meleager and Atalanta, from cartoons by Le Brun, for Monsieur, the brother of Louis XIV. Mr. Guiffrey writes much more and in the most flattering terms of this family, but I have translated enough to thoroughly substantiate their high position in the tapestry world. Translating from the same book, I read that : " Henry Rydams began his career as tapestry weaver in 1629, and was succeeded in 1671 by his son who bore the same name as his father." After reciting some of the remarkable series woven by these artists, Mr. Guiffrey adds " the descendants of the Rydams, allied with the descendants of the Leyniers, preserved their atelier until the middle of the XVIII century. There are some tapestries which bear the names of both of these celebrated families." This series of Judith and Holofernes is one of these rare series, as it " bears the names of both these celebrated families." Henry Rydams was the author and signer of one-half of this series, as Everard Leyniers was of the other half.

In Vol. XLVIII of the MSS. still preserved in the

Barberini Library, there is an inventory of the tapestries owned by the nephew of Pope Urban VIII—the Cardinal Charles Barberini—dated October 25, 1695.

In this Inventory, the series Judith and Holofernes is designated as follows :

" Series woven in silk and wool representing the history of Judith—8 tapestries."

These 8 tapestries were bought directly of the Princesses Barberini, through the advice and assistance of the writer, and have therefore never been in the hands of any European antiquity dealer, but are absolutely Virgin tapestries, which have not been submitted to any alteration or cutting whatever, consequently they are now in all respects, excepting some trifling repairs, exactly as they were when they left the ateliers of Leyniers and Rydams.

The writer desires to emphasize the importance and value of these advantages, because so many of the tapestries one finds for sale in the antiquity shops of Europe, have been bereft of their original borders, which have been replaced by modern ones far less ornate in design and far more ordinary in execution, whilst many others have been darned or patched instead of repaired after the manner of the original weaving.

Notwithstanding the writer's long residence abroad and the many and important acquaintances and friendships which he made in Europe, it would have been impossible for him or any other foreigner, to have obtained the permission of the Italian Government for the exportation of the renowned Barberini Collection of tapestries, and this permission was therefore procured by the powerful friends and connections of the Princesses Barberini. The experts chosen by the Italian Minister of Public Instruction to examine the collection, reported that all the series of tapestries ranked as works of art, consequently the tax of 20 per cent required by the Italian Government on the exportation of antique works of art from Rome, has been paid on every one of the series comprising this collection. To each tapestry the Italian Minister of Public Instruction has affixed his official seal, as evidence that the Government has not only consented to its exportation, but that the Pacca or export tax on it as an antique work of art has been paid. Without these seals the tapestries would have been stopped at the frontier by the Custom House authorities, and not allowed to leave Italy, and the would-be exporters would have suffered other disagreeable consequences, both financial and personal.

All the principal newspapers of the Kingdom published an account of the sale of the collection, and many bewailed the loss of the art treasures in sorrowful and indignant language, whilst others demanded that the Government should reprimand the officials who had permitted their exportation.

By the assistance of his friends, some of whom are in the Direction of the Royal galleries of the Uffizi at Florence, the writer had every one of the Barberini tapestries examined by the experts of those renowned galleries, and had affixed to each one the seal of the Uffizi in further recognition of their great artistic value and as further identification that they have paid the export tax heretofore mentioned. Consequently, each tapestry bears two seals, and upon the lining of several there is a curious design in India ink, the purport of which the writer has not yet discovered.

To sum up, these tapestries, inasmuch as they represent Biblical subjects, are more suitable for public museums, libraries or galleries, than they are for private residences. They are Rubenesque in character, and were woven in the ateliers of two of the most celebrated families of tapestry weavers that Flanders ever produced. They are full of sentiment, strong in character, the principal personages are in general superbly drawn. Judith is personified in almost all with a wonderful fidelity to the Apocryphal account in the early editions of the Old Testament of her character and acts. In fact, it is easy to read on the faces of all the emotions or passions which control them. In addition, they are especially remarkable for their wondrously harmonious coloring: nowhere is there any jarring, even the borders and the subjects possess the same general tones, and your eyes are charmed with their delicately blending shades, softened by age. The artists who created the cartoons exhibited talents of the highest order in the surprising homogeneity of the varied details, constituting each composition, and in the remarkably readable visages of the prominent actors. Those who interpreted the cartoons possessed not only long experience and great skill, but that subtle instinct or talent for harmony in color which gives tapestries their wonderful warmth, decorativeness and sumptuousness. These tapestries were all rated as antique works of art by the experts of the Italian Government and those of the Royal galleries of the Uffizi. In addition to the superior artistic merits just designated, they are unusually fine in tissue, and possess the historic distinction of having belonged for about 250 years to the great patrician family of Pope Urban VIII, the Barberini of Rome, and were included in the inventory of the tapestry possessions of Cardinal Carlo Barberini in 1695. They are in first class order, have never been mutilated in any way, and are absolutely in the same condition, excepting some trifling repairs, as when they issued originally from the ateliers of Leyniers and Rydams.

In conclusion, they are splendid specimens of Flemish tapestries of the last half of the XVII century, and were woven whilst Flanders stoutly maintained her struggle for leadership with France, and before the wise laws and better pay of the French Monarchs had robbed her of nearly all her best men and caused the downfall of her prolonged pre-eminence in textile painting.

Monograph on the Series Diana.

Composed of Seven Tapestries.

Title and Size of each Tapestry.

No. 20.—Diana stringing her bow.
  Height 13 feet 6 inches.   Width 10 feet 11 inches.

No. 21.—Diana wounds a satyr.
  Height 13 feet 5 inches.   Width 17 feet 2 inches.

No. 22.—Nymph lacing the sandals of Diana.
  Height 13 feet 3 inches.   Width 19 feet 5 inches.

No. 23.—Woman nursing a child.
  Height 13 feet 7 inches.   Width 13 feet.

No. 24.—Two women fleeing from a dragon.
  Height 13 feet 6 inches.   Width 13 feet 2 inches.

No. 25.—Warrior killing a dragon.
  Height 13 feet 6 inches.   Width 15 feet 4 inches.

No. 26.—Man and woman walking in a garden.
  Height 13 feet 5 inches.   Width 15 feet 2 inches.

Origin, History and Importance.

These tapestries were woven in Brussels at the close of the XVI or beginning of the XVII century, in the ateliers of Jacques Geubles and Jean Raes, who were among the most celebrated master weavers of their time. The mark of Brussels in Brabant, BUB, is woven in the bottom galon of every one, and the monograms of the authors are woven in the dexter galon of every one, that of Raes in the top and that of Geubles in the bottom part.

Muntz prints on pp. 373 and 375 of "*La Tapisserie*,"

fac-similes of the monograms of Jacques Geubles and Jean
Raes which are the exact counterparts of those woven in
these tapestries, and he states in another part of the same
work that the signature of the former appears on a " History of Diana " belonging to a private collection.

Both the families to which these chefs d'atelier belonged received commands for tapestries from the greatest
and most enlightened potentates of Europe, which is con-
vincing testimony in favor of the importance and artistic
value of their productions.

The emperor Charles V commanded of the early members of the families Geubles and Raes a series of the
" Sermons of the Apostles " and a series of the " Acts of
Apostles," the latter after the renowned cartoons of
Raphael.   Both of these series now adorn certain apart-
ments in the royal palace at Madrid and part of each bears
the monogram of Raes, and part that of Geubles.   The
series " History of Decius," which is now preserved at
Vienna amongst the textile treasures of Austria, is signed
in part by Jacques Geubles the younger and in part by
Jean Raes the younger.   The cartoons for the last named
tapestries were painted by Rubens, all of them were en-
graven by Schumzer, and seven of them now hang in the
gallery of Prince John of Lichtenstein in Vienna.   This
nobleman owns also four of the tapestries, the Church of
Saint-Etienne possesses two, and the balance decorate the
chateau of Prince of Auersperg.   It is said that Prince
Albert of Solms-Braunfels owns replicas of the whole series.

François Raes the elder was Doyen of the Brussels
tapestry guild in 1554.   About 1550 he wove, in collaboration with William Pannemaker, the series " Triumphs of

the Gods " after Mantegna which are now in the National
Garde-Meuble at Paris, and about 1557 with the same
collaborator the series " History of Noah " now in the
Palace at Madrid. He was arrested by order of the Inqui-
sition when the Duke of Alva was Governor of the Netherlands, but fortunately succeeded in escaping from prison
and the torture chamber and most probably from martyr-
dom. François Raes the younger was author of the grand
series " Alexander the Great " which was exposed in Paris
in 1874 at the Exhibition in the Champs Elysees and which
created great enthusiasm.

The tapestries which are the subject of this monograph
were woven by the second generation of master weavers
in the families Geubles and Raes on order most probably
for Louis XIII of France, since they formed part of
those presented by him to Cardinal François Barberini
when Legate at the French Court, and since every one
bears the signature of both these master-weavers. It is
unusual to find all the tapestries in any series regularly
signed, and more unusual to find them all signed by both
the artists collaborating in their production. Consequently
it is fair to presume that unusual circumstances surrounded
the creation of this series. In addition the character of
the subjects, as is explained at greater length later on,
indicates that they were intended to represent episodes in
the life of an ancestor of Louis XIII. On the death of
Jacques Geubles the elder, his widow, Catherine Van den
Eynde, not only succeeded to the management of his
atelier, but maintained the high standard of work for which
it was celebrated. The Archduke Albert of Austria, who
was one of the most enthusiastic admirers and collectors

of textile paintings in the XVII century, commanded not less than forty tapestries of her between the years 1605 and 1613, and among them were eight which illustrate a " History of Diana " or " Diana the Huntress," and which now form part of the Royal collection of Spain. Jean Raes the elder was, according to Alphonse Wauters in " *Les Tapisseries Bruxelloises*," associated with her in the production of these series and also in that entitled " History of Noah." She died in 1629, leaving an imperishable name in tapestry literature, and was succeeded by her son Jacques Geubles the younger who was Doyen of the tapestry guild in Brussels in 1626 and 1627 and died in 1637.

There is a tapestry in the Palace of the Prince of Chimai-Caraman in the Belgian capital which represents " A King combatting a lion " and in which is woven the following inscription :

DIVINO PALLADIS ARTE

PICTURAM SUPERAVIT

AGUS

That is to say, " Thanks to the divine art of Pallas the broche* surpasses painting." The chef d'atelier who thus haughtily declared the supremacy of textile paintings over those in oils, was the above mentioned Jacques Geubles the younger.

Jean Raes the elder was the head of one of the most important ateliers ever established in Brussels. He filled several high municipal positions in that city between 1617 and 1634, and finally became its Burgomaster. In collaboration with Geubles he wove two series of tapestries

_____
*The instrument used in weaving tapestries.

illustrating the Acts of the Apostles. The first was after the cartoons of Raphael, and the second is declared by some authorities to be a replica of the first in so far as the central compositions are concerned, but others insist that it illustrates another conception of the same subjects by Rubens. The description of the borders of the second, as printed in the catalogue hereafter named, makes it certain, however, that they are far and away less important and less artistic than those of the first. The second series is nevertheless of extraordinary artistic importance since part of it brought nearly $8,000 per tapestry at auction in 1877. It was woven for the Archduke Albert about 1595 and was presented in 1620 to the Carmelites of Brussels, and finally became incorporated in the collection of the Dukes of Alva. Among the celebrated productions of the joint ateliers of Raes and Geubles is the series " History of the Trojan War," which formed part of the renowned collection of the Dukes of Alva when it was sold in Paris at the Hotel Drouot in 1877, as did also the second series of the Acts of the Apostles heretofore mentioned. In the same collection, and sold at the same time as the preceding, was a magnificent piece by Jean Raes, the elder, with 51 figures, representing the " Coronation of Charlemagne."

The illustrated catalogues of the objects of art comprised in the aforesaid sale contain reproductions of some of the most important tapestries in the collection, among which are several of those woven by the elder Raes and Geubles. The Royal Palaces of Spain contain several series from the ateliers of the Raes family, in addition to the Acts and Sermons of the Apostles, heretofore men-

tioned. Among them are the " History of Theseus," the
" Labors of Cupid," the " History of Absalom," and the
" History of Decius."

The learned Benedictine monks, Marténe and Durand,
in writing of the tapestries representing the " Acts of the
Apostles," woven to all appearance in the ateliers of the
Raes family for the Abbey Church of St. Peters in Ghent,
state in substance that it is believed the cartoons for them
were painted by Raphael ; that when he had finished these
designs, he had done nothing more delicate with his brush
than that which the master weaver had done with his
broche ; that the estimated value of the ten pieces was
20,000 florins ; and that it was said a Governor-General
of the Netherlands had offered 100,000 florins, a sum
equal to $250,000 of our money, for replicas of them.
These tapestries were woven in 1556, remained in the
church of St. Peters until they were removed to Amster-
dam on the approach of the armies of Louis XV, and were
finally sold in 1821 to England.   It is more than probable
that Charles I secured the renowned cartoons of Raphael,
which now hang in the South Kensington Museum, from
the descendants of Jean Raes, and that they did not dis-
pose of them until they had abandoned all hopes of reaping
any additional advantages from reproducing them in tapestries, for it must be remembered that there were woven
during the XVI and XVII centuries some thirty-six series
of the " Acts of the Apostles."

The Geubles and Raes were the authors of many
other remarkable series, but the writer has enumerated
enough to convince anyone that the tapestries woven in
their ateliers rank amongst the most valuable and impor-

tant that were produced in Flanders during the palmiest days of her textile supremacy.

When Cardinal Barberini decided, early in the XVII century, to found a manufactory of tapestries in Rome, he requested some of the great prelates of the Romish Church, particularly in France and Flanders, to gather for his guidance all the information in their power concerning the place of origin and character of the raw materials employed, the methods of dyeing, the processes of weaving, the skill and talents of those directing the most important ateliers, and all else that would be of service to him. The Flemish prelate, who made the most elaborate and instructive report of all, stated among other things that " the best masters in tapestry weaving are Jean Raes, François Van Cotthem, Jean Raet, the widow Geubles, and Bernard Van Brustom, and the leading wool dyer is Daniel Leyniers." No higher honor could have been paid Raes and Geubles than to include their names in the short list of those who led the Flemish weavers in the manufacture of tapestries at the period when their products outrivalled those of any other part of the world.

By an edict of Charles V promulgated in 1528 all the master-weavers in Brussels were obliged to weave the mark BUB in the tapestries issuing from their ateliers. Consequently all those which bear this mark were made subsequently to that date, and are the only ones which are incontestably of Brussels origin.

Although there have been several ingenious reasons advanced for the incorporation of a design like the figure 4 in the initials or monograms of several of the great master-weavers of Flanders, yet none of them have been accepted as conclusive, and consequently the cause for it continues a mystery.

On pages 72 to 77 of the MSS. XLVIII in Vol. 141 preserved in the Barberini Library, there is, among other things, the following statement, which the Chevalier Zenuti of Florence copied for the writer, and of which the latter inserts a verbatim translation :

" Account given by the learned Luca Holstenio of the Barberini tapestries with prices, commencing with those which include the History of Constantine the Great, Artemisia, Rinaldo, Diana, &c., presented by the most Christian King, Louis XIII of France to Cardinal Barberini, Legate to France, 1625."

Since the tapestries composing the series Diana, which is the subject of this monograph, were acquired of the Barberini family, this extract proves that they were presented by Louis XIII to Cardinal François Barberini. This fact alone entitles them to rank amongst the most historically important tapestries in existence.

Eugene Muntz, Conservateur of the Library and Archives in the Beaux Arts at Paris, and the author of several standard works on tapestry, published, in 1874, copious extracts from the aforesaid MSS., in the " *Revue des Societes Savantes*," 5th Series, Vol. VII, pp. 504 to 520, and stated in his preface that, in addition to those he copied, there exist in the Barberini Library, " other documents which contain the description of the Gobelins given Cardinal Barberini by Louis XIII and the Gobelins, on sale, which were offered him." It was from these " other documents " that the Chevalier Zenuti made the extract hereinbefore translated and introduced.

All the tapestries composing the series described in this paper were bought in the Barberini Palace without the assistance of any intermediary. The stamped monogram of Cardinal François Barberini (F. B.) and that of the Cardinal Antonio Barberini, made up of the initial letters C. A. B., and his cardinal's hat and Maltese cross were visible upon the canvas backing of most of these tapestries when taken from the Palace, as were also the words Cmo. Sig. Cardinale Antonio Barberini.

They are absolutely virgin specimens of antique textile art, have not had their colors touched up nor renewed in any fashion, have not been submitted to any alteration nor cutting whatever, and are consequently in all respects, excepting some trifling repairs, exactly in their original condition, as delivered from the ateliers of Jacques Geubles and Jean Raes.

It is but just that these unusual and important advantages should be recognized and enlarged upon, because so many of the tapestries offered for sale in Europe have been darned or patched instead of repaired after the manner in which they were originally woven, or have had their colors renovated by the application of paints, or have had their original borders removed and replaced by modern ones of far less ornate design and of far more ordinary execution.

Description of the Borders.

They consist of a beautiful design in sepia upon a deep red background. This design is composed of architectural foliage in arabesque formation, interspersed with satyrs, bacchantes and fauns. In each top corner of the sinister

borders appears a winged female bust and in each bottom
one a squatting satyr. The same positions in the dexter
borders are decorated respectively with a winged male bust
and a squatting bacchante. In the centre of each top and
bottom border is a pedestal bearing the armless bust of a
satyr, supported on both sides by satyrs, bacchantes and
fauns. The whole effect is exceedingly rich and striking.

Description and Prominent Artistic Merits of each Tapestry.

In the first tapestry (No. 20) Diana strings her bow facing
the spectator. Her imposing figure is grandly drawn and magnificently attired. She bears a quiver of arrows upon her
back and the crescent shines amidst the plaits of her hair.
She wears, over a bluish gown of striped and lustrous silk,
a superb mantle of rich and changeable colors, embroidered
with varied and peculiar designs. The graceful folds and
wonderful colors of the mantle, and the beautiful sheen on
the silken gown are marvels of textile art. The face is
evidently a portrait, for such eyes, with their cold, severe, and
haughty expression, must have been painted from life.
They follow the observer from point to point as he moves
to and fro in front of them. Two handsome and finely
drawn dogs attend their mistress, one lies upon the ground,
with only its head and fore paws visible, and the other stands
at her side and gazes into her face. Some of her nymphs
bathe in the stream which flows through the centre plan,
and others sport amongst the trees in the right field. The
landscape scenery is soft in color, and artistically devel-

oped. The yielding bank of mossy turf upon which the huntress stands, the clear flowing water, and the barks and foliage of the trees have been interpreted with surprising fidelity to nature. The whole composition is bathed in a soft light which shimmers through the trees, glances from their leaves and the costume of Diana, brightens the surface of the water, and barely touches the ground.

In the second tapestry (No. 21) Diana sits upon a mossy mound at the base of a tree on the banks of a flowing stream. She wears, over a blue robe, a wonderfully rich mantle, similar in design and character to that worn in the preceding tapestry but worked in more brilliant colors. Her queenly figure is superbly drawn and gracefully posed. Her head, adorned with the crescent, rises with patrician dignity from her shoulders. Her sensitive, dreamy eyes gaze upon the spectator, no matter from what direction he views them. Her quiver of arrows lies upon the ground at her side and a kneeling maid laces the strings of her sandals. Half way up the mountain in the far background are the ruins of some antique buildings. In the centre plan two camels browse upon the hillside, the dogs of Acteon rend their unfortunate master, and Diana and her maids fly towards their sanctuary in the grotto under the hillside. Through the open arches we catch a glimpse of their canopied beds, and of a nymph at her toilet. In the woods above the grotto is a rural banquet scene, where the guests surround a table spread within a summer-house roofed with vines. The architecture in the distant background, and the stream which winds its way through the whole landscape, around the trees behind Diana, where a wildcat holds a lamprey in its mouth, and between her and the grotto, where a fish sports in the water, give remarkable depth to the composition. The splintered stump, the characteristic bark and foliage of every different tree, the variegated vines and leaves, the water in the sluggish stream and the mossy ground, were not only interpreted by a master hand but by one who loved and studied nature in her varying moods and forms.

In the third tapestry (No. 22) Diana lowers her bow and turns her face from a bearded satyr whom she has wounded with an arrow. The poor fellow has raised an arm as if to parry the weapon, but without avail. An affrighted hare watches her movements from its hiding place beneath some branches and leaves in the foreground. She wears the same blue robe beneath the same superb mantle as in the preceding tapestry, although it appears richer because it is draped differently and a greater amount of it is exposed to view. A quiver of arrows is fastened at her back, and the crescent adorns her hair. Her majestic figure is capitally drawn and splendidly posed. Her pensive, dreamy eyes gaze apparently into futurity, and express neither pride nor pleasure, but rather regret at the death wound she has inflicted. In the background to the left are the ruins of two antique buildings, before one of which a group of men and women gather round some game lying dead on the terrace. One man defends it from the dogs, ready to devour it, by beating them back with sticks. In the foreground to the left are some broken bits of architecture with lizards creeping in and out between them. In the quiet background scene a church and other buildings nestle among the trees. The distant view of forest and water, the near-by foliage heralding the approach of winter, and the vines and turf, in fact all the landscape features, are woven in soft, delicate and exquisitely harmonized colors. The whole composition is daintily gilded with the mellow light of an autumnal afternoon.

In the fourth tapestry (No. 23) a fine looking woman nurses a child, with a bow, an attribute of Diana, lying upon the rug at her side. Her stately figure is well drawn and posed with unaffected dignity. She wears, over a delicate rose colored gown, a blue mantle richly embroidered with peculiar designs which probably represent the armorial bearings of some distinguished family. She sits upon a terra-cotta rug, beneath a dark blue canopy ornamented with stripes, and stretched between the columns supporting the crumbling arches of an ancient temple. It is weighed down in the middle by the hide of a leopard, whose head and paws dangle over its edge. The right field is occupied by a foaming, rushing stream, down which serpents, broken column and statuary are impetuously carried. The center plan shows two women, one of whom struggles to escape from the other, who has seized her by the hair, and the feet of a statue which have withstood the shock of the waters. The summits of the mountains in the background are covered with the ruins of temples and other antique buildings. The foreground is decorated with a vase filled with rich, ripe fruit, a glass goblet half full of wine, and a variegated lizard, which has sought a place of safety from the roaring torrent. The light and shade effects have been admirably managed, from the strong glow bathing the woman and child, illuminating the mountain tops and glancing from the marbles and the canopy, to the soft hues beneath the arches and in the recesses of the temple. The perspective features have been treated with equal ability by crowning the mountains with architecture and circling the ruins of the city from the central plan to the foreground, and twisting the stream through the right field from the base of the mountains to the steps of the temple. The variegated marbles in the architecture, and the rich, carved decorations in the arches and on the dado, have been reproduced with signal success.

The principal personage is a puzzle. The leopard's skin and the bow indicate Diana herself, which the nursing babe apparently belies. Mythology, however, informs us that Diana not only punished mothers who abandoned their children, but succored their offspring. It is possible, therefore, that the subject was intended to demonstrate these episodes in her legendary life, and that even amidst ruins and chaos, she chastised heartless mothers and nursed their babes. Notwithstanding this possibility, it seems more reasonable to conclude that it represents, under the guise of the goddess, some great lady who was renowed for her charities, inasmuch as the compositions of the fifth, sixth and seventh tapestries preclude the belief that they were woven to illustrate any part of the mythological history of the goddess Diana.

In the fifth tapestry (No. 24) two women flee from a dragon. The nearest one is the heroine of the series, judging by her mantle and by the sleeves of her gown. They certainly have reason to be terrified by the menacing aspect of the beast as he rears upon his hind legs and threatens them with his savage claws, fiery eyes, open mouth and forked tongue. He is a magnificent but ferocious looking animal, with golden breast and belly, bluish bristles on muzzle, neck, and back, gorgeous wings full of eyes and armed with

pointed ribs, many jointed and variegated tail, and webbed
feet covered with shaded scales. The two women are well
drawn and move rapidly as is shown by the swirl of their
robes and mantles. The mossy turf upon which they run
actually appears to yield beneath their weight. Although
the colors of their picturesque costumes harmonize beautifully with those in the dragon, yet there is everything else
but harmony in the feelings and purposes of the pursuer
and pursued. The marshy border of the stream, the yellow
scum upon the water, the trees, foliage, and distant fields,
have, like the mossy turf, been interpreted with rare skill
and judgment.

Inasmuch as the boat in which they cross the stream in
the second plan is poled by a man, it is impossible, judging
by the fate of Acteon, to believe that either of the women
represents the goddess Diana.

In the sixth tapestry (No. 25) a majestic warrior has
wounded the dragon which terrified the women in the preceding tapestry, and his athletic attendant withdraws one of the
arrows, which has penetrated its body beneath the upraised
wing. Its dying agonies have been developed with remarkable ability, particularly in the despairing eyes, the stiffening
tail, the powerful leg, which convulsively straightens in
death, and the gigantic wings still outstretched in a last
effort to escape. The principal personage is unquestionably a portrait from life. The features are not those of
an idealized model, but of a man painted as seen in flesh
and blood by the cartoonist. His casque is ornamented
with huge ostrich feathers. He wears a picturesque mantle, similar in character and colors to those worn by Diana,
but embroidered with different designs. It is gracefully

draped across his shoulders and about his body, over a richly decorated coat of mail.   He carries a bow in his hand, and a quiver of arrows is strapped on his back.   Although his outstretched hand betokens satisfaction with the work he has done, yet his eyes appear to read into futurity rather than gloat with joy over his victory.

The beginning of the fight is capitally delineated in the centre plan to the right, and to the left a river, spanned by a bridge of masonry, winds its way towards the horizon. The ruins of an antique building crown the hilltop in the distant background.   Both men exhibit energy and movement, and are capitally drawn and finely posed.   The colors of their costumes and those of the dragon harmonize admirably.   Indeed the reddish tones in general and the red hose of the attendant in particular, distract the eyes from the blood which must of necessity be shown as flowing from the terrible wounds of the animal.   A soft steady light pervades the whole composition.   There are scarcely any strong hues, excepting those in the costume of the warrior.   Everywhere else the tones are warm and dark, or delicately shadowed by the approach of twilight.

In the seventh tapestry (No. 26) a man and a woman promenade in a garden.   He evidently explains some project to her as they walk along with his arm around her waist.   They are an imposing looking couple, well drawn and royally attired.   She wears over an elegant, orange-colored robe, embroidered with designs mostly in red, a beautiful green tunic of striped and lustrous silk, decorated with a large and set pattern.   He wears a full beard, and over a brown and red tunic, a rich yellowish mantle, draped across his left shoulder and tucked under his girdle in front.   It is evident from the graceful movements of the flowing parts of their costumes that that there is a stiff breeze blowing, and that the authors of the tapestry knew how to summon even the elements to their aid in this impressive exhibit of their talents and skill. The landscape represents a French garden, laid out in methodical form, decorated with a fountain, and surrounded in part by a balustrade. An open promenade, with a vine covered roof supported by termini, partly encircles the little lake at the base of the mountains. The roof of the marble entrance to this promenade is decorated with vases of leaves and fruit. The spandrels of the large marble arch in the garden where three people are at work, are adorned with designs principally representing "Abundance." Its top is crowned with a vase of leaves and fruit and a couple of reclining figures. The well developed landscape scene of rising hills, studded with chateaux and divided by stretches of stone walls, proves better than words that the authors were masters of all the laws of perspective. The yielding bank of mossy turf, and the slow flowing rivulet are among the additional charms of this interesting and highly decorative tapestry. The light is diffused with equal strength throughout the entire composition.

Four Flemish Renaissance Tapestries.

These tapestries were woven in Brussels near the middle of the XVI century in the atelier of William de Pannemaker who was one of the most renowned of that pleiad of Flemish master-weavers who made the name of their country famous throughout the civilized world.

The mark of Brussels, Brabant, is woven in the bottom galon and the monogram of William de Pannemaker in the dexter upright galon of part of them.

William de Pannemaker was the author of that remarkable series consisting of 12 tapestries which represent the "Conquest of Tunis" by the Emperor Charles V and which are now preserved by Spain in the Escurial at Madrid among the choicest of her art treasurers. The cartoons were painted by Jean Vermeyen of Flanders who accompanied the Emperor in that war and made his initial designs on the spot. This wonderful series is known everywhere and although Pannemaker wove several others of great importance, yet it is not worth while to enumerate them all, for this one alone sufficed to place him at the head of his profession even in Flanders. It may be of interest, however, to mention the two series " Vertume and Pomona," one of which is in the Escurial at Madrid, and the other, with the same subjects but enclosed in entirely different borders, is in this country, having previously formed part of the Barberini Collection. In the production of this grand series as well as in that of the "Apocalypse," also at Madrid, Pannemaker, although he was personally the principal author of both, had two collaborators whose monograms are woven in the dexter upright galons of certain pieces. It is more than probable that he had the same collaborators in the production of the Flemish Renaissance Series now on view in this exhibition.

Guiffrey, the Director-General of the Gobelins, declares that " the series ' Conquest of Tunis ' and ' Vertume and Pomona ' are justly considered among the most beautiful specimens of the ancient Brussels ateliers," and that " these grand works bear witness to the boundless reputation of William de Pannemaker whose place is marked in the Pantheon of the celebrated Brussels master-weavers beside that of Peter de Pannemaker and Peter Van Aelst." It will be remembered that the latter was the author of the glorious series " Acts of the Apostles " now in the Vatican which were woven for Pope Leo X after the cartoons of Raphael, and that the former was the author of the " Life of Christ " now at Madrid, the cartoons for part of which were painted by Van Orley, although they were for some time attributed to Rogier Van der Weyden.

No. 27.—Height 14 feet 7 inches. Width 12 feet 9 inches.

In this tapestry a large body of cavalry, armed with spears and with banners flying, march across the centre plan in front of their three chiefs who occupy the left foreground. The background is filled with bodies of both cavalry and infantry on opposite sides of a stream.

The infantry are drawn up in battle array but make no effort to dispute the passage of the cavalry and the lot of camels and elephants across the stream by the three bridges thrown over it, which forces the conclusion that the whole composition represents the manœuvres of an army rather than the beginning of a battle.

No. 28.—Height 13 feet 8 inches. Width 13 feet 8 inches.

In the foreground of this tapestry a man has raised a heavy club studded with iron points, to strike a huge sea-lion which, spouting water, attempts to climb up a bank towards a woman who starts to run away in alarm. The left foreground and centre plan are filled with hunting scenes; the near background discloses a French chateau and garden, and the whole far background consists of hillsides covered with trees and a range of bald mountain peaks.

No. 29.—Height 14 feet 9 inches. Width 12 feet 10 inches.

This tapestry illustrates a battle scene. In both the first and second plans a lot of cavaliers, some on foot and some on horseback, engage in deadly conflict. Several have already been stretched upon the ground but the others continue the struggle with unabated vigor. One poor knight in the second plan leans backward on his horse in agony as his antagonist plunges a spear into his body. Another knight, in the immediate foreground, is on the point of transfixing his fallen opponent with his spear. The peculiar device upon each of the different shields indicated its owner at that epoch to his friends and foes as clearly as his coat of arms.

No. 30.—Height 10 feet 11 inches. Length 12 feet 7 inches.

This tapestry illustrates a dual scene. In the centre plan a number of ladies and gentlemen, partly on foot and partly on horseback are hunting with falcons and dogs. In the left foreground three women have grouped themselves around a basket of flowers. This group probably represents the companions of Proserpine when she was carried off by Neptune who whirls through the air in his chariot and horses on a bank of clouds with his unwilling captive in the dexter upper corner. The whole background consists of a landscape scene dotted with chateaus and gardens. This is a peculiarly interesting tapestry, not only for the character of its composition and the different subjects illustrated, but for the life and movement of the hunting party, and the grief and dismay manifested by the companions of Proserpine, particularly by the one who has thrown her arms wide apart. This tapestry does not belong to the same series as the preceding, as is evident by the dissimilarity in the borders and in the size of the personages represented, although it was woven at the same epoch and illustrates people clad in costumes of the same age. The border is narrower, the bouquets of flowers are smaller, and it is totally different in that the individual subjects in the centres of the horizontal and upright borders are enclosed in medallion shaped cartouches.

All four of these tapestries are remarkable for their soft and delicate colors; for their delicious background scenes; for their grand perspective qualities; for their magnificent men and women, clad in rich and picturesque costumes; and for the varied and attractive subjects included in their

borders.   These borders are of unusual width and are
divided by architectural motives and bouquets of flowers
and fruits into several compartments each of which represents an independent scene.   In fact they are marvels of
textile art, for they exhibit a wonderful luxuriance of motives, exquisitely developed, skilfully combined, and woven
to form, if such an expression is allowed, symphonies in
color.

The Achilles Series.

Composed of Two Tapestries.

Enriched with Gold and Silver Threads.

No. 31—Height, 13 ft. 7 in.   Length, 15 ft. 4 in.

It represents a priest, attired in a rich robe, about to
sacrifice a lamb upon the altar in the centre field.   He is
attended by two acolytes each of whom carries a flaming
lamp.   In the right field stands a woman and her child.
She carries a vase and evidently offers it and the pile or
vases, etc., in the centre foreground as gifts to the god or
goddess to whom the sacrifice is offered.   The right border
consists of a female caryatid, with a Minerva-like head,
carrying a shield on which appears the head of Medusa.
The left border consists of a male caryatid, with a Jove-
like head.   In the top border there are cherubs, holding
festoons of flowers and fruits, and a cartouch enclosing a
Latin inscription designating the subject illustrated in the
tapestry.

No. 32—Height, 13 ft. 6 in.   Width, 13 feet.

It represents a king with a scowling face, sitting on a
throne chair and looking savagely at a youth standing in the
left field who is in the act of drawing his sword.   There
are three men in the right field, one of whom places his
hand in that of the king as if to restrain the latter's anger.
In the centre foreground there reclines a huge and superbly
drawn lion.

The right border consists of a female caryatid, with two snakes coiled round its base and spitting and hissing at each other. The left border consists of a male caryatid blindfolded and with chains hanging over the mantle enclosing its torso.

In the top border there are cherubs, holding festoons of flowers and fruits, and a cartouch enclosing a Latin inscription designating the subject illustrated in the tapestry.

These tapestries were woven in Flanders during the first half of the XVII century, in the atelier of the celebrated Jean Van Leefdael whose signature appears in the bottom galon of the second one. The fame of this master spread throughout the whole tapestry world and many of the most remarkable tapestries of the XVII century which now adorn the museums and palaces of Europe, issued from his atelier, and that of his son Guillaume Van Leefdael. Among those in this country which owe their origin to him is the well-known series of " Cleopatra and Mark Antony " now in the Metropolitan Museum of New York.

The tapestries which are the subject of this sketch are remarkably fine examples of decorative art. The figures are colossal to be sure but they are well drawn, full of vigor and character, and chef d'oeuvres of the epoch of production. The lights and shades have been admirably managed and the perspective treatment shows equal skill and experience. The features of the principal personages are almost all extraordinary. It is fair to presume they were drawn from life inasmuch as they are unusually natural. The tapestries have been repaired to a certain extent, but most fortunately these repairs are largely in the upper parts above the personages and in the accessory designs, and therefore do not injure the originality nor diminish the artistic importance of the personages.

It was a happy thought to introduce carytides supporting the roofs of the porticos under which the scenes represented are enacted, for they not only make uncommon, and exceedingly effective borders, but they contribute largely to the perspective effects of both compositions.

The Series Meleager and Atalanta.
Composed of Three Tapestries, two of which are exhibited.

Mythological History.

Meleager was the son of Œneus, whom Bacchus had initiated in the culture of the vine plant, and in the production of wine. His mother was Althæa, granddaughter of the god Mars. At the birth of Meleager, Queen Althæa consulted the Parcæ or Fates as to the length of his life, and was warned by them that as soon as the billet or brand of wood, which was then burning on the hearth, should be entirely consumed, Meleager would die. The affrightened mother seized the burning brand, extinguished the fire upon it, and carefully concealed it. By this act she rendered her son invulnerable.

Atalanta was the daughter of Iasius, King of Arcadia. Her father desired a son, and was so indignant at the birth of a daughter that he heartlessly exposed his infant to death in the forest. She was suckled by a she-bear, until discovered by some hunters, who named her Atalanta and reared her. Naturally she followed the chase with ardor and devotion, and developed into a magnificent and courageous woman.

The names of Meleager and Atalanta are indissolubly associated in the renowned hunt of the Calydonian boar, and the recital of the causes and results of that classical event would clearly depict the subjects of these tapestries. At a harvest festival King Œneus neglected to pay the usual honors to Diana. The indignant goddess, to punish him for the slight, sent a ferocious boar of enormous size, to ravage the fields of Calydon. No ordinary mortals were capable of killing the terrible beast, so the Aetolians besought Meleager, the King's son, who inherited the prowess of his ancestor, the god Mars, and who was endowed with invulnerability, to undertake the perilous task. The magnitude of the danger can best be appreciated by recalling the names of the celebrated heroes summoned by Meleager to assist him. They were the renowned Theseus, the fierce Jason, the brothers Castor and Pollux, Peleus, the father of Achilles, Telamon, the father of Ajax, the wise Nestor and the superb Atalanta. In the " Meleager " of Euripides there is a full account of the arms and appearance of all the heroes present at this renowned hunt. They agreed that the head and hide of the boar should be the trophy of the one who slew it. After nine days of feasting, all the assembled guests prepared for the chase and soon discovered the savage beast in his lair, amongst the reeds in a marshy strip of ground. Jason threw his spear, but in its flight Diana removed its point, and the boar, uninjured, assailed Nestor, who was obliged to seek safety in the branches of a large tree. Telamon in his impetuosity stumbled and fell, but an arrow from Atalanta pierced the boar's hide and drew the first blood. It was a slight wound, but Meleager proclaimed it with delight. Anceus, excited by envy, loudly defied both the boar and Diana, and rushed towards the infuriated beast, but was quickly slain by it. The lance of Theseus, although thrown with desperate strength, glanced on the bough of a tree and failed to reach its object. Meleager, after one unsuccessful effort, thrust his spear into the boar's side, inflicting a serious wound; he then drew his sword and with repeated strokes finally killed it. The other hunters crowded around him, congratulated him, and proclaimed him entitled to its head and hide, but, through his love for Atalanta, he declared that both belonged to her since she had given the savage beast its first wound, and notwithstanding the protests of some, he cut off its head and presented it to her, as is illustrated in the first tapestry. On her return to Arcadia, Phlexippus and Toxeus, uncles of Meleager and brothers of Althæa, assailed her and forcibly robbed her of the trophy under the pretext that if Meleager resigned it for himself, he could not do so for the rest of the family. Meleager, furious at the wrong done the maiden he loved, forgot the ties of kindred, fiercely attacked his uncles, tore the boar's head from them and killed them both, as is illustrated in the second tapestry. When Althæa repaired to the temples to offer sacrifices for the victory of her son over the Calydonian boar, she learned of the terrible fate of her brothers, and by whose ha they had been slain. With frenzied haste she changed her "garments of rejoicing for those of mourning." Grief at the loss of her brothers coerced her into desiring to revenge their death upon her son. In despair she lifted from its place of concealment the fateful brand, with which destiny had linked his life and commanded her attendants to prepare a sacrificial fire. "Four times she essayed to place the brand upon the pile; four times draws back shuddering at the thought of bringing destruction upon her son. Now she is pale at the thought of the purposed deed, now flushed with anger at his act, but the sister finally prevails over the mother," and a prey to conflicting emotions, she thrust the brand into the fatal fire, as is illustrated in the third tapestry. It "gave, or seemed to give, a deadly groan," and the unfortunate Meleager was seized on the instant with sudden and serious illness. As the fire consumed the brand his sufferings weakened him, and when it was reduced to ashes his body was a lifeless corpse. Remorse drove Althæa to suicide, and Diana, taking pity on the uncontrollable grief of the sisters of Meleager, metamorposed them into birds.

Series Meleager and Atalanta.

Composed of 3 tapestries, enriched with gold and silver threads.

No. 33.—Not here exhibited. Meleager presents Atalanta
with the head of the Calydonian boar.
Height 11 feet 4 inches. Width 10 feet, 1 inch.

Meleager partly kneels upon the body of the huge
animal, as he offers Atalanta its head. In his left hand he
holds upright a short and heavy sword; behind him an
attendant, with a long javelin in his right hand, holds the
dog of his master in leash. Atalanta is seated beneath a
tree, under a drapery suspended from its branches. She
extends one hand towards Meleager, and the other rests
upon her bow. Behind her are three of her maids, and at
her right a young huntress, with a quiver at her back,
shows unmistakable joy at the honor shown her mistress.
The dogs of Atalanta lie near her feet.

This tapestry, unfortunately, has not yet been brought
to America, so a photograph of it is exhibited.

No. 34.—Meleager attacks and kills his uncles.
Height 11 feet 4 inches. Width 10 feet 7 inches.

Meleager has overtaken his uncles at the edge of a
forest, and successfully struggles to recover the boar's
head, of which they had forcibly deprived Atalanta. One
is already mortally wounded and lies dying upon the
ground; the other, astride the body of his fallen brother,
vainly endeavors to retain possession of the trophy which

Meleager has seized with his right hand, whilst with his left he is about to plunge his sword into his antagonist. Atalanta, with horror stricken countenance, flies from the scene.

No. 35.—The Mother of Meleager thrusts the fatal brand into the fire.

Height 11 feet 5 inches.   Width 7 feet 10 inches.

Queen Althæa raises her mantle to shield her eyes from the sight of her unnatural crime as she abandons to the flames the billet of wood, upon the preservation of which the life of her son depended. The fire is built upon a sacrificial altar, with three legs and claw feet, which is placed in front of a term or column, surmounted with the bust of a scowling satyr. The avenging goddess Tisiphone, whose head, with hair entwined with serpents, appears amidst the smoke, has seized the wrist of the Queen and prevents her from withdrawing the fatal brand from the flames.

These tapestries were woven in Brussels, after the cartoons of Le Brun, in the third quarter of the XVII century, by G. Van der Strecken, Doyen of the Guild of tapestry weavers, whose signature is woven in the bottom galon of one of them. The engravings of these cartoons can be seen in the Cabinet of Engravings in the National Library at Paris, and have been compared with these tapestries so as to verify the statement that the latter are interpretations from the original cartoons of Le Brun. Another series was woven in the Gobelins for the Duke of Orleans, and is now preserved in the Garde-Meuble at Paris. The borders are of unusual beauty and wonderful richness in design, consisting of flowers, fruits and leaves, swords, spears, bows, quivers of arrows, horns, helmets, plumes, live and dead game, urns and brands mingled in remarkable artistic purity. One of the aforesaid engravings illustrates these magnificent borders alone without any interior subject, in the place of which, however, are engraved the following words:

> "TAPESTRIES
> OF
> HIS ROYAL HIGHNESS
> MONSEIGNEUR THE DUKE OF ORLEANS,
> REPRESENTING
> THE HISTORY OF MELEAGER
> DESCRIBED IN THE 8TH BOOK OF THE METAMORPHOSES OF OVID.
> EXECUTED AFTER THE CARTOONS OF THE ILLUSTRIOUS
> CHARLES LE BRUN,
> CHIEF ARTIST OF THE KING OF FRANCE.
> ENGRAVED BY THE DIRECTION AND UNDER THE SUPERVISION
> OF B. PICART,
> M.D.C.C.XIV."

The costumes of the principal personages represented are richly charged with gold and silver threads. When the opulent nobles and rich families of France sacrificed their gold and silver objects of art, and plate to the depleted treasury of Louis XIV, the use of these costly threads in tapestries was discontinued. Consequently even if they were unsigned it would be evident that this series was made prior to these sacrifices. The fineness of their tissue, their wealth of gold and silver threads, the evidence that they are interpretations from the original cartoons of Le Brun, and the celebrity of the atelier from which they issued, establish that they were made for a great prince like the Count of Artois, or for one who had a semi-royal exchequer and who could control cartoons belonging to the crown.

To sum up, the borders are marvellously beautiful in

character, technique, and harmony of color; the composition of each tableau is strong, life-like and full of action, the personages represented are superbly drawn and skillfully grouped, each face clearly portraying the emotions which control its owner; the colors are soft and delicate, have been admirably selected and harmoniously blended so that the figures melt delightfully into the landscape backgrounds. The tapestries are of the finest quality and the best workmanship, were woven in a glorious era of art, in a celebrated atelier, after cartoons by a great master, and consequently rank among the most important cabinet specimens of antique Flemish tapestry weaving in existence.

No. 36.—Queen Cleopatra summoned before Augustus Cæsar.

Height. 10 feet 6 inches.   Length, 14 feet 6 inches.

This tapestry was woven in Flanders during the last quarter of the XVII century and represents Cleopatra attended by her maids of honor appearing before Imperial Cæsar and his suite.   All the figures are gracefully drawn, richly costumed and skilfully grouped.   Cleopatra carries a fan of ostrich feathers.   Cæsar wears the costume of a Roman general and two pages carry the train of his mantle.

The tragic end of the Queen after her unavailing attempt to fascinate and enthrall the mighty emperor is too well known to require comment, but at the same time, the romantic halo which hovers over every work of art portraying any episode in the life of this unfortunate and capricious Queen invests it with additional attractions.

The tapestry is unusually decorative and picturesque in

general effect, is woven in soft, harmonious colors, and the
landscape background makes a charming foil to the interesting group in the foregroud.

No. 37.—The coronation of the King.

Height, 12 feet 7 inches.   Length, 12 feet 5 inches.

This tapestry was woven in Flanders during the last
quarter of the XVII century and is part of a number
which decorated the Buonsignori palace of Sienna, Italy,
for more than a century.

The king, with arms crossed upon his breast, kneels
upon a cushion and has laid his helmet upon the step
near him. Behind him stand a black page and three
Asiatic looking officers, one of whom holds a banner over
him. The Priest or Emperor performing the act of coro-
nation stands upon the steps of a palace and is supported
by three ministers or courtiers.

Tradition states that the subject represented is "Charle-
magne crowning one of his feudatories."

The composition is attractive and well developed, the
colors of the tapestry are soft and harmonious, and it is a
picturesque and exceedingly decorative specimen of Flemish art.

No. 38.—King Solomon Tapestries.

Height, 9 feet 6 inches.   Length, 12 feet 2 inches.

King Solomon, seated on his throne, leans forward and
crowns the Queen of Sheba. He wears a crown and carries a
sceptre, and she is attended by four maids of honor.

No. 39.—Battle Scene in King Solomon's time.

Height, 10 feet 6 inches.   Width, 10 feet 3 inches.

A conquered King, standing outside the gates of his
vanquished city, tenders his crown to King Solomon, who

refuses to accept it. The soldiers continue fighting in the background, a couple of horsemen are engaged in deadly contest in the second plan, and a despairing officer throws himself upon his sword in the foreground.

These tapestries were woven in Lombardy, Italy, during the last quarter of the XVII century. They are worthy of study on account of the excellence of their compositions, their harmonious colors, softened by time, their graceful drawing, the sympathetic beauty of the Queen and the manly strength and power of the male personages.

No. 40.—Carnival Scene in Venice.

Height, 12 feet 9 inches. Width, 9 feet 9 inches.

This tapestry was woven in Italy in the last quarter of the XVII century. In the foreground two persons in rich costumes point at two women and a man who appear at the window of a tower. Two officials stand at the foot of the tower evidently consulting whether their duty requires them to investigate what is going on above which so deeply interests all the spectators particularly the gaping boy.

In the centre of the top border is a crown and other paraphernalia of a sovereign Prince.

It is fine in texture and its colors are rich and well preserved. The beautiful twisted and fluted columns which form the lateral borders indicate the nationality of the author of the cartoon and materially add to the attractiveness of the main composition.

No. 41.—The Toilet of Venus.

Height 9 feet 6 inches. Width 7 feet 9 inches.

This tapestry is of French origin and was most probably woven at Beauvais during the first quarter of the

XVIII century after a cartoon inspired by Boucher. The goddess of Love has just descended in her car from Olympus upon a bank of clouds. She is attended by her emblematic turtledoves and by the gods of Love and Hymen, the latter bearing his lighted torch. She has alighted upon a grassy mound adorned with flowers over which she has thrown her rich red mantle, and a little cupid presents her with a golden apple as she steps into the stream of water which flows, laden and scented with flowers, from an urn upon which a river nymph reclines. The tapestry is surrounded with a conventional border largely made up of architectural foliage and other characteristic designs. Venus is a model of beauty and loveliness as she gracefully reclines upon one knee and arm and enjoys in advance the delicious luxury of a bath. She takes no notice of the little cherub offering the apple, nor of the two others floating on the bank of clouds, but dreamily watches the rippling water. The gods of Love and Hymen, on the contrary, intently follow all her movements. The huge cloud which has borne her to earth floats away in the distance and partly envelops her as well as the river nymph, the attendant gods and the doves. This tapestry is a veritable work of art, as it is the product of a master's hand. The composition is thoroughly Boucher in style and character, the colors are soft and delicate, the flowers are exquisitely moulded and shaded, the water is absolutely transparent, and the personages are artistically drawn and their flesh tints are admirably reproduced.

A Brief Account of the Antiquarians of the Art Institute.

In the year 1877 several ladies residing in Chicago met in the house of Dr. R. N. Isham and organized the Chicago Society of Decorative Art.

The objects of the Society were "to create in this community a desire for artistic decoration and for a knowledge of the best methods of ornamentation; to provide training in artistic industries, and enable decorative artists to render their labor remunerative." In the year 1888 these aims had been so far accomplished that the members did not feel the necessity of keeping up the active work of the Society, and therefore the purely business interests were disposed of. The Society desired to affiliate itself more closely with the Art Institute, and in 1891 it was resolved to devote its funds and influence to the collection of antiquities in pottery, china, embroideries, laces, etc., to be presented to the Art Institute.

At the annual meeting held in November, 1894, it was resolved to change the name of the Society to one which should more nearly express the object which it now has in view, and the title adopted was The Antiquarians of the Art Institute.

All ladies who desire to help in this work of adding museum articles to the already beautiful collection, are invited to join this association by sending $5 to the Treasurer, Mrs. Dudley Wilkinson, 163 Rush St., who will return ticket granting all privileges of the association.

Catalogue of Articles Presented by the Antiquarians to the Art Institute.

MINIATURE.—Artist unknown, donor unknown. Nucleus of the present collection, 1890.

COLLECTION OF ECCLESIASTICAL EMBROIDERIES.—Spanish. Conventional designs, embroidered in silk floss, outlined with gold on silver tapestry cloth, seven pieces.

> Three vestments, 16th century;
> One chasuble, 17th century;
> One cope, 17th century;
> One banner, 18th century;
> One band, 17th century.

COLLECTION OF FOURTEEN ANTIQUE FANS.—French and English. 18th century and early part of 19th century.

DIVAN AND PILLOW COVERS.—Persian. Blue silk studded with brass ornaments.

ARCHBISHOP'S SEDAN CHAIR.—Spanish. 17th century. Frame is of carved wood, gilded, exterior covered with elaborate embroidery, silk, gold thread and horse hair, upon cream-white satin.

CHALICE VEIL.—17th century. White silk, embroidered in colors. Presented by Mrs. John N. Jewett.

ANTIQUE CRIMSON AND GOLD SILK DRESS.—Worn by a Hindoo woman.

> Presented by Mrs. Mahlon Ogden.

TURKISH JACKET.—Embroidered in gold, worn in the Royal Harem, Cairo.
>Presented by Mrs. A. A. Sprague.

PAIR BROCADE SLIPPERS.—With silver buckles, worn by Sybil Prout when presented at the court of Charles II of England.
>Presented by Mrs. S. I. Hurtt, New York.

BAPTISMAL MANTLE.—Blue silk brocade, used in the family of Baron Prout, of England, from about the year 1670 to 1842.
>Presented by Mrs. S. I. Hurtt, New York.

ONE YARD POINT D'AIGUILLE LACE.—15th century.
>Presented by Mrs. Charles Emerson, Concord, Mass.

GREEK ARCHBISHOP'S MITRE.—Byzantine. 16th century. Embroidered in pearls and jewels.

BISHOP'S MITRE, 15TH CENTURY.—Scarlet silk, embroidered in gold thread and seed pearls.

SILVER KORAN HOLDER.—18th century.

LEATHER BOOK COVER.—18th century.

ONE SILVER COFFEE CUP HOLDER.

TWO BRASS COFFEE CUP HOLDERS.—18th century.
>Presented by Dikran G. Kelekian.

Purchased from the Columbian Exposition.

CRIMSON AND CREAM BROCADE.—Italian. (Milan.) Beginning of the 17th century.

GREEN BROCADE.—Italian. Called "eyes of the tiger," beginning of the 15th century. Only a few pieces remaining, which belong to museums in Europe.

YELLOW BROCADE WITH SILVER.—Italian. Beginning of 16th century.

GREEN BROCADE.—Italian. (Venice.) End of 16th century.

RHODES EMBROIDERY.—17th century.

PAIR KURDISH LADY'S BOOTS.—18th century.

BROCADE BELT.—Persian. 17th century, with gold and silver threads.

PAIR OVERSHOES.—18th century.

EMBROIDERED VELVET.—Italian. (Genoa.) Beginning of 15th century.

VELVET.—French. 15th century. The other half is in the Art Museum of Berlin.

PERSIAN EMBROIDERY.—17th century.

EMBROIDERED SHOES.—Persian. 17th century. Silver heel pieces.

TWO PIECES PERSIAN EMBROIDERY.

EMBROIDERY.—Spanish. (Grenada.) 14th century.

EMBROIDERED BAND.—French. 16th centnry.

VELVET.—European. 17th century.

LEATHER BOOK COVER.—With silver threads. 18th century.

PAIR WOODEN SHOES.—With silver ornaments. Turkish.

AJOUR BAND.—Spanish. 16th century.

PEARL STUDDED BELT WITH BUCKLES.

BOOK COVER.—Green satin embroidered.

COPE.—Italian. (Venice.) 18th century. Embroidered in silver and silk floss. Belonging to the family of Sessler Morosino Bisselle.

TABLE COVER.—Italian. 15th century. Brocatello with border of appliqué and embroidery.

PORTIERE OF CRIMSON VELVET.—Italian. (Genoa.) 17th century. Family coat of arms embroidered in the centre, border in appliqué.

1894.

STOLE.—Japanese. 17th century. Tea brown silk, brocaded in colors.

STOLE.—Japanese. Late 17th century. Olive green silk, brocaded in colors. Design of dragons.

STOLE.—Japanese. Early 18th century. Blue silk, ornamented with scroll work in colors.

STOLE.—Japanese. 18th century. Red silk, brocaded in green, gold and white.

NO-KYOGEN ROBE. Japanese. Early 18th century. Flower cart pattern, brocaded in many colors.

PRIEST'S VESTMENT.—Japanese. 18th century. Shokko design woven in colors.

ALTAR CLOTH.—Japanese. Late 18th century. Tea brown silk with geometric design in gold and colors.

JIMBAORI (PARADE SURCOAT).—Japanese. Late 18th century. Dark blue silk, with design of dragons woven in colors.

TEMPLE HANGING. — Japanese. Pre-restoration time. Chrysanthemums (imperial crest) on upper part of hanging. Solid embroidery of antique style, with brocade trimmings.

CABINET.—Spanish. 16th century. Exterior ornamented with gilded ironwork, inlaid with ivory within and without.

WEDDING GOWN.—Japanese. Golden age. Silk warp, gold thread filling, brocaded with plum twigs and blossoms.

EMBROIDERY.—East Indian. Three bands of striped silk alternating with four wider bands of white linen, embroidered with flowers.

Presented by Mr. H. H. Getty.

LADY'S CLOAK.—East Indian. Scarlet cloth, embroidered in white silk.

SCARF END.—Persian. 18th century. Blue camels hair.
           Presented by Mrs. John J. Glessner.

COAT AND WAISTCOATS.—Formerly the property of and worn by Marshal Ney, 1769-1815. Coat of plum color velvet, embroidered. Waistcoats of white silk, embroidered. Presented by Mrs. T. B. Blackstone.

VELVET PURSE.—French. 17th century. Embroidered in silver. Duplicate in South Kensington Museum, London.   Presented by Mrs. John N. Jewett.

PRIEST'S ROBE.—Spanish. White silk embroidered in colors.   Presented by Mrs. E. S. Stickney.

BROCADE.—Japanese. Blue silk embroidered in gold.
           Presented by Mrs. S. E. Barrett.

COLLECTION OF ITALIAN BROCADES.—
     Green Brocade with gold and silver designs;
     Crimson Brocade with gold and color designs;
     Cloth of gold brocaded in pale pink.
           Presented by Mr. C. L. Hutchinson.

1895.

COLLECTION OF BROCADES AND LACES.—Italian. 13th to 18th century. 713 pieces.
           Presented by Mr. Martin A. Ryerson.

EMBROIDERY.—Italian. Part of a head dress.

ANTIQUE LACE.—Venetian. Rose point.

ANTIQUE LACE.—Valenciennes.
           Presented by Mrs. Sumner Ellis.

FAN.—English. 17th century. Carved ivory; painting believed to be by Sir Joshua Reynolds.

ARCHBISHOP'S CROSIER. 17th century. Silver repoussé.

PLATE.—Spanish. 17th century. Talavera ware.

BLUE JAR.—Spanish. 17th century. Talavera ware. Arms of the Bishop of Toledo.
> Presented by Mrs. F. H. Gardiner.

BRUSSELS LACE.—Court Ruffles and Jabot formerly belonging to George II, 1680.

ANTEPENDIUM OR ALTAR FRONTAL.—Egyptian. 12th century. Woven of flax.

VELVET HANGINGS.—Genoese. 15th century. Color the rare ruby called "pigeon blood."

CAVALIER'S DRESS.—18th century. Brown plush embroidered. White satin waistcoat.

LACE.—Flemish. 17th century.

KORAN.—Antique.

EMBROIDERED CLOTH.—From Tomb of Rameses I.
> Obtained from Museum of Boulak.

SHELL FAN.—17th century.

FAN.—French. 18th century. Carved ivory inlaid with gold.
> Presented by Mrs. H. O. Stone.

TWO PIECES ANTIQUE EMBROIDERY.—Figures on white satin. Framed.
> Presented by Prof. and Mrs. Wm. Gardiner Hale.

WEDDING COFFER. — Florentine. Carved gilt with painted panels. Presented by R. Hall McCormick.

SCARF OF PINEAPPLE CLOTH.—Embroidered. Brought
from China about 1840.
> Presented by Mrs. Geo. Higginson, Jr.

HOLY WATER CUP.—Florentine. End of 16th century.
Style of Cellini. Background of gilt bronze. Figures
of Virgin and Child of Silver. Frame of carved
wood.   Presented by Mrs. J. Y. Scammon.

FOUR PIECES LACE.—Sicilian.

THREE PIECES EMBROIDERY.—Saracenic.

ONE PIECE EMBROIDERY.—Italian. On white silk.

ONE PIECE EMBROIDERY.—Early French. On canvas.

MEXICAN IDOL.—Gold.

BRONZE LAMP.—Naples. Antique.

ONE ROMAN MEDAL.

TWO ROMAN COINS.—Bronze. Anicetus Pont. M. 155
A. D.; Gregorius IIII, Pont M. 827 A. D.

ONE SILVER COIN.—Gregorius II, Pont. M. 715 A. D.
> Presented by Mrs. J. Y. Scammon.

PRIEST'S OVER ROBE.—Japanese, early 18th century. Red
satin, brocaded in colors.

PRIEST'S UNDER ROBE.—Japanese, early 18th century.
Green corded silk. Both worn by Buddhist High
Priest.   Presented by Mrs. Chas. N. Pope.

GOLD HEAD DRESS.—Holland. Antique. Worn in province
of Friesland.

EMBROIDERED ROBE.—From Manila, Phillippine Islands.
Pine apple cloth, embroidered by natives. Five
yards long. Exhibited at London Exposition, 1851.
Presented by Mrs. J. W. Scott, Mrs. George E. Adams,
Mrs. George Bass, Mrs. Charles R. Crane, Mrs. John C.
Coonley, Mrs. Samuel E. Gross, Mrs. Walter L. Peck,
Mrs. George Sturges.

List of Members.

Adams, Mrs. Cyrus H.
Adams, Mrs. George E.
Adsit, Mrs. Charles C.
Allerton, Mrs. S. W.
Andrews, Mrs. Irene F.
Armour, Mrs. Philip D.
Austin, Mrs. Frederick C.
Avery, Mrs. Frank M.
Ayer, Mrs. B. F.
Ayer, Mrs. E. E.

Baker, Mrs. Alfred L.
Baker, Mrs. F. H.
Barbour, Mrs. Edward
Bannard, Mrs. Henry C.
Barnes, Mrs. Charles J.
Barrett, Mrs. S. E.
Bartlett, Mrs. A. C.
Bartlett, Miss Florence
Bausher, Mrs. Henry
Beach, Mrs. Myron H.
Beckwith, Mrs. Corydon
Beidler, Mrs. William H.
Bellas, Mrs. Thomas
Birch, Mrs. Hugh T.
Blackstone, Mrs. T. B.
Blair, Mrs. Chauncey J.
Blair, Mrs. Henry
Blair Mrs. Lyman
Blair, Mrs. William
Blatchford, Mrs. E. W.
Boal, Mrs. Chas. T.
Boal, Miss

Bodman, Mrs. L. W.
Bowen, Mrs. Joseph T.
Bradwell, Mrs. Thomas
Brega, Mrs. Chas.
Briggs. Mrs. David C.
Broomell, Mrs. G. D.
Buckingham, Miss Kate S.
Burley, Mrs. Arthur G.
Burrows, Mrs. Thomas
Burton, Mrs. Stiles
Bush, Miss Emma
Byram, Mrs. Augustus

Carpenter, Mrs. A. A.
Carpenter, Mrs. George A.
Carpenter, Mrs. W. O.
Carmichael, Mrs. G. S.
Cary Mrs. Wm. H.
Cass, Mrs. G. W.
Caton, Mrs. Arthur J.
Chalmers Mrs. Wm. J.
Chandler, Mrs. Frank
Chapman, Mrs. J. D.
Chapman, Miss Emma
Chappell, Mrs. C. H.
Cheney Mrs. Charles E.
Clark, Mrs. A. E.
Clayton, Mrs. E. P.
Coburn, Mrs. Lewis L.
Cochran, Mrs. J. L.
Coffin, Mrs. C. H.
Conger, Mrs. Wm. P.
Conover, Mrs. Chas. H.

Coolidge, Mrs. F. S.
Coonley, Mrs. John C.
Cooper, Mrs. J. S.
Cramer, Mrs. Ambrose
Crane, Mrs. C. R.
Crane, Mrs. Richard T.
Crawford, Mrs. Henry
Crawford, Miss
Crosby, Mrs. F. W.
Culver, Mrs. Chas. E.

Dana, Mrs. A. P.
Delano, Mrs. F. A.
Dent, Mrs. Thomas
Dewey, Mrs. A. B.
Dickinson, Mrs. Melissa
Dunham, Mrs. J. H.
Dunham, Miss M. V.

Eames, Mrs. Henry F.
Eddy, Mrs. Arthur J.
Ellis, Mrs. Sumner
Ellsworth, Mrs. James W.
Elmes, Mrs. Chas. T.
Eltonhead, Mrs. E. Y.
Emerson, Mrs. Ralph

Fargo, Mrs. Charles
Fargo, Mrs. Charles Evelyn
Farnsworth, Mrs. George
Farwell, Mrs. A. L.
Farwell, Mrs. Chas. B.
Farwell Mrs. John V.
Field, Mrs. Samuel G.
Fisher, Mrs. Walter L.
Fitz-Simons, Mrs. C.
Forsyth, Mrs. H. H.
Frank, Mrs. Henry L.
Freer, Mrs. L. C. P.
French, Miss

Fuller, Mrs. Henry T.
Fuller, Mrs. Percival

Gage, Mrs. Lyman J.
Galt, Mrs. A. T.
Gibbs, Mrs. C. S.
Givins, Mrs. Robt. C.
Glessner, Mrs. John J.
Glessner, Miss Frances
Goldsmith, Mrs. A. L.
Goodman, Mrs. W. O.
Goodwin, Mrs. Artie
Goodwin, Mrs. Daniel
Gorton, Mrs. Frank S.
Grey Mrs. William L.
Grey, Mrs. John
Greene, Mrs. Augustus W.
Greene, Mrs. Horatio N.
Gregory, Mrs. Robert B.
Gross, Mrs. Samuel E.

Hambleton, Mrs. C. J.
Hambleton, Miss M. G.
Hambleton, Mrs. Earl L.
Hamill, Mrs. Chas. D.
Hamill, Mrs. Ernest A.
Hamline, Mrs. John H.
Haskell, Mrs. F. T.
Hays, Miss Mary
Healy, Mrs. G. P. A.
Helmer Mrs. Frank A.
Hempstead, Mrs. Marcia
Henderson, Mrs. C. M.
Henderson, Mrs. W. S.
Henrotin, Mrs. Chas.
Herrick, Mrs. John J.
Hesing Mrs. Washington
Hibbard, Mrs. Wm. G.
Higginson, Mrs. Geo. Jr.
Hill, Mrs. Henry L.

Hinde, Mrs. Thos. W.
Hjortsberg, Mrs. Max
Holman, Mrs. Alfred
Howland, Mrs. Walter
Hoyt, Mrs. Wm. M.
Huddleston, Mrs. Kate G.
Hunt, Mrs. Robt. W.
Hutchinson, Mrs. B. P.
Hutchinson, Mrs. Charles L.
Hyde, Mrs. James Nevins

Isham, Miss
Isham, Miss Frances
Isham, Mrs. Ralph N.

Jacobs Mrs. B. F.
Jamieson, Mrs. Egbert
Jenkins, Mrs. John
Jewett, Mrs. John N.
Johnson, Mrs. Oliver K.
Jones, Mrs. Daniel A.
Jones, Mrs. J. M. W.
Jordon, Mrs. C. H.
Jordon, Mrs. Cady Morrow
Jordon, Mrs. Scott
Judah, Mrs. Noble B.

Keen, Mrs. E. H.
Keep, Mrs. Albert
Keep, Mrs. Chauncey
Kelley, Mrs. David
Kelley, Mrs. William E.
Kennedy, Mrs. Madison B.
Kendall, Mrs. B. W.
Kenly, Mrs. D. F.
Kerfoot, Miss Alice G.
Kerr, Mrs. Wm. R.
Kimball, Mrs. Mark
Kimball, Mrs. W. W.
Kimball, Mrs. Edward A.

King, Mrs. Henry W.
Klapp, Mrs. Wm. H.
Knott, Mrs. Henry A.
Kohlsaat, Mrs. H. H.
de Koven, Mrs. John

Laflin, Mrs. Geo. H.
Laflin, Mrs. Louis E.
Laing, Mrs. J. R.
Lancaster, Mrs. Eugene A.
Landon, Miss
Lathrop, Mrs. Chas. D.
Lawson, Mrs. Victor F.
Lay, Miss
Levi, Mrs. Henry C.
Linn, Mrs. W. R.
Lombard, Mrs. J. L.
Loomis, Mrs. J. Mason
Loss, Mrs. C. E.
Lyon, Mrs. John B.

MacVeagh, Mrs. Franklin
McBean Mrs. A. J.
McCagg, Mrs. E. B.
McClurg, Mrs. A. C.
McCullough, Mrs. H. R.
McCormick, Mrs. Cyrus H.
McCormick, Mrs. R. Hall
McKay, Mrs. James, R.
McVicker, Mrs. J. H.
Mandel, Mrs. E.
Marsh, Mrs. Wm. Dixon
Manierre, Mrs. Geo.
Marshall, Mrs. Caleb H.
Martin, Mrs. Horace H.
Martin, Mrs. Elmer
Mather, Mrs. A. C.
Matthews, Mrs. C. L.
Matthews, Mrs. E. S.
Mayer, Mrs. Levy

Meachem, Mrs. C. O.
Michelson, Mrs. Margaret H.
Mitchell, Mrs. Lewis B.
Mitchell, Mrs. W. H.
Moore, Mrs. Wm. H.
Morgan, Miss Anna
Moss, Mrs. Wm. Lathrop
Mott, Mrs. John G.
Mulliken, Mrs. Alfred H.
Mulliken, Mrs. Chas. H.
Munson, Mrs. Chas.

Nelson, Mrs. Walter C.
Nevers, Mrs. Edward
Nickerson, Mrs. Roland
Nickerson, Mrs. S. M.
Nixon, Mrs. Wm. K.
Norwood, Mrs. Fred W.

O'Brien, Mrs. W. H.
Ogden, Mrs. Mahlon
Oglesby, Mrs. Richard J.
Otis, Mrs. Frederick R.
Otis, Mrs. Geo. L.
Otis, Mrs. Joseph E.
Owen, Mrs. J. R.

Palmer, Mrs. Potter
Papin Mrs. F. S.
Partridge, Mrs. C. W.
Parker, Mrs. A. A.
Pearce, Mrs. J. Irving Jr.
Peck, Mrs. Clarence I.
Peck, Mrs. Walter L.
Pettibone, Mrs. A. G.
Pettibone, Mrs. P. F.
Pike, Mrs. Eugene S.
Poole, Mrs. Abram
Porter, Mrs. H. H.
Potter, Mrs. Orrin W.

Potwin, Mrs. W. S.
Pullman, Mrs. Geo. M.
Pullman, Miss

Quincy, Mrs.

Raymond, Mrs. Chas. L.
Ream, Mrs. Norman B.
Ream, Miss Frances
Ream, Miss Marion
Revell, Mrs. Alex. H.
Robbins, Mrs. Henry S.
Roberts, Mrs. K. E. P.
Rogers, Mrs. J. M.
Rogers, Miss S. C.
Roloson, Mrs. R. W.
Root, Mrs. John W.
Rosenfeld, Mrs. M.
Roys, Mrs. Cyrus D.
Ryerson, Mrs. Martin
Ryerson, Mrs. Martin A.
Runnells, Mrs. John S.
Rutter, Mrs. David

Scammon, Mrs. J. Y.
Schlesinger, Mrs. L.
Scott, Mrs. James W.
Scott, Mrs. R. S.
Scribner, Mrs. Sandford A.
Sheldon, Miss P.
Sheldon, Mrs. G. W.
Shortall, Mr. John G.
Skinner, Miss
Skinner, Miss Frederika
Sloan, Mrs. Alice
Smith, Mrs. Byron L.
Smith, Mrs. Ernest F.
Smith, Mrs. Fred A.
Smith, Miss Irene
Smith, Mrs. Orson

Snow, Miss Helen
Spoor, Mrs. John A.
Sprague, Mrs. A. A.
Sprague, Miss
Stanbro, Mrs. S. D.
Stevens, Mrs. Frank L.
Stevens, Mrs. Plowden
Stevenson, Mrs. Alex. F.
Stickney, Mrs. E. S.
Stone, Mrs. H. O.
Stone, Mr. Melville E.
Stone, Mrs. Melville E.
Swan, Mrs. J. H.

Thomas, Mrs. Theodore
Tolman, Mrs. S. A.
Tree, Mrs. Lambert
Trimmingham, Miss
Trippe, Mrs. M. G. W.
Trude, Mrs. Alfred S.
Turner, Mrs. V. C.
Tyler, Mrs. F. C.

Ullman, Mrs. Frederick
Upton, Mrs. Edw.

Van Schaick, Mrs. A. G.

Waite, Miss Ella R.

Wait, Mrs. Horatio L.
Walker Mr. Edwin
Walker, Mrs. Edwin
Walker, Mrs. Geo. C.
Walker, Mrs. J. M.
Walker, Mrs. James Ransom
Walker, Mrs. Wm. B.
Walker, Mrs. W. S.
Waller, Mrs. Robert
Waller, Mrs. Edward C.
Walsh, Mrs. John R.
Walter, Mrs. J. C.
Watkins, Mrs. E. T.
Weidner, Mrs. R. F.
Wentworth, Mrs. Moses J.
Wheeler, Mrs. Ezra I.
Wheeler, Mrs. Geo. Henry
Whitehead, Mrs. E. P.
Whitehouse, Mrs. Meredyth
Wilkins, Mrs. Jos. E.
Wilkinson, Mrs. Dudley
Williams, Miss Anna P.
Williams, Miss Cornelia B.
Willing, Mrs. Henry J.
Willing, Miss
Wilmarth, Mrs. H. M.
Wilson, Mrs. J. P.
Wilson, Mrs. Milton H.
Worthington, Mrs. E. S.